SELECTED PRAISE FOR *IDEAS ARE FREE*

"In [this] groundbreaking book.... Robinson and Schroeder have a message for today's overburdened, stressed-out managers and supervisors: the solution to your problems is closer than you realize—it lies within the people who work for you."
    —The American Management Association (AMA)

"One of the thirty best business books of the year."
    —Soundview Executive Book Summaries

"*Ideas Are Free* is the definitive book on getting—and applying—business-transforming ideas from frontline employees."
    —Society for Human Resource Management (SHRM)

"*Ideas Are Free* shows how a good idea has no bounds and how pursuing such ideas is the essence of everyone's job today. Robinson and Schroeder outline a workable plan for tapping into this unlimited resource and harnessing its potential."
    —Bob Nelson, PhD, bestselling author of *1001 Ways to Reward Employees* and *1001 Ways to Take Initiative at Work*

"*Ideas Are Free* is a must-read for every manager. Robinson and Schroeder provide an invaluable blueprint of how to unlock one of the great assets that is frequently untapped in business—employee ideas."
    —Richard A. Goldstein, Chairman and CEO, International Flavors and Fragrances, Inc.

"This is the quintessential book on how to foster and leverage free ideas from employees. It's a must-read for any project manager responsible for delivering programs designed to increase sales, increase productivity, increase customer satisfaction, and increase company employee morale. Read it today. Use it tomorrow."
    —Brand Autopsy

"*Ideas Are Free* is a refreshingly insightful book that managers at all levels should read. It spells out how to take advantage of your most valuable asset—the combined intellectual capital of all of your people."
    —Donald V. Fites, Former Chairman and CEO, Caterpillar, Inc.

"*Ideas Are Free* sets out a roadmap for totally integrating ideas and idea management into the way companies are structured and operate. Robinson and Schroeder show how to take advantage of this virtually free, perpetually renewing font of innovation."
    —Society of Manufacturing Engineers

"Wherever you sit in the hierarchy, read *Ideas Are Free* to seize powerful ideas about potential gains for your organization's progress and prosperity."
    —Lead Well Institute

"Ideas Are Free does a terrific job of capturing the extraordinary benefits of effective 'idea generation processes' that unleash the total people power of any organization that strives for excellence."
    —Tom Malone, President and COO, Milliken & Company (Winner of both the Malcolm Baldrige National Quality Award and the European Quality Award)

"You have an opportunity to make major improvements in your business by following the basic guidelines set forth in this book. I rate this book 5½ stars, a first in this category. It's that powerful. (Only the Bible and the Constitution receive 6 stars.)"
    —Paul Tulenko, PhD, Syndicated Small Business Columnist, Scripps-Howard

"Throw out employee suggestion boxes (they don't work – and never have). Think twice about dangling monetary rewards to workers whose ideas save the company money (the pitfalls are numerous; moreover, it's not necessary). These are just two of the surprising yet well-documented messages in *Ideas Are Free...*"
    —*American Way,* American Airlines' in-flight magazine

IDEAS ARE FREE

IDEAS ARE FREE

How the Idea Revolution Is Liberating People and Transforming Organizations

Alan G. Robinson
Dean M. Schroeder

BERRETT-KOEHLER PUBLISHERS, INC.
San Francisco

Berrett-Koehler Publishers, Inc.
235 Montgomery Street, Suite 650
San Francisco, CA 94104-2916
Tel: (415) 288-0260   Fax: (415) 362-2512   www.bkconnection.com

ORDERING INFORMATION

Quantity sales. Special discounts are available on quantity purchases by corporations, associations, and others. For details, contact the "Special Sales Department" at the Berrett-Koehler address above.

Individual sales. Berrett-Koehler publications are available through most bookstores. They can also be ordered direct from Berrett-Koehler: Tel: (800) 929-2929; Fax: (802) 864-7626; www.bkconnection.com

Orders for college textbook/course adoption use. Please contact Berrett-Koehler: Tel: (800) 929-2929; Fax: (802) 864-7626.

Orders by U.S. trade bookstores and wholesalers. Please contact Publishers Group West, 1700 Fourth Street, Berkeley, CA 94710. Tel: (510) 528-1444; Fax (510) 528-3444.

Production Management: Michael Bass Associates

Berrett-Koehler and the BK logo are registered trademarks of Berrett-Koehler Publishers, Inc.

Printed in the United States of America

Berrett-Koehler books are printed on long-lasting acid-free paper. When it is available, we choose paper that has been manufactured by environmentally responsible processes. These may include using trees grown in sustainable forests, incorporating recycled paper, minimizing chlorine in bleaching, or recycling the energy produced at the paper mill.

Library of Congress Cataloging-in-Publication Data

Robinson, Alan (Alan G.)
   Ideas are free: how the idea revolution is liberating people and transforming organizations / Alan G. Robinson, Dean M. Schroeder.
     p. cm.
   Includes bibliographical references and index.
   ISBN-10: 1-57675-282-8; ISBN-13: 978-1-57675-282-1 (alk. pap.)
   ISBN-10: 1-57675-374-3; ISBN-13: 978-1-57675-374-3 (pbk.)
   1. Suggestion systems. 2. Management—Employee participation.
3. Organizational change. 4. Organizational effectiveness. 5. Corporate culture. I. Schroeder, Dean M. II. Title.

HF5.549.5.S8R63   2003
658.3'14—dc22
                                         200362804

First edition 2004; first paperback edition 2006
10 09 08 07 06   10 9 8 7 6 5 4 3 2 1

To Margaret, Phoebe, and Margot

To Kate, Lexie, Liz, and Tori

CONTENTS

CHAPTER 7

———■————————

GETTING MORE AND BETTER IDEAS   169

CHAPTER 8

———■————————

LIBERATION AND TRANSFORMATION   197

Performance expectations for managers keep going up. Managers are continually asked to do more, but to do it with less. For top management, the standard response to flagging profits and increasing competition has become budget cuts and layoffs. Middle managers and supervisors suffer the consequences, as they are left with too few resources and people to do the work. They are forced to operate in survival mode, putting in long hours to deal with an endless stream of urgent problems. Almost never do they have the time to think beyond this month's results. In addition, they are under constant scrutiny, and their jobs are not secure.

Ironically, help is closer than they realize—in the people who work for them. They are the ones who *do* the work, and they see many things their managers don't. On a daily basis, they see what is frustrating customers, causing waste, or generally holding the organization back. Employees often know how to improve performance and reduce costs *more intelligently* than their bosses do. Yet they are rarely given a chance to do anything about it. No one asks them for their ideas.

Over the last century, many managers have recognized the huge potential in employee ideas and tried to tap it. But few have been truly successful. Those few found that they had fundamentally changed their organizations and helped them reach extraordinary levels of performance. Today, most managers either don't realize the full power of employee ideas or have never learned how to deal with them effectively. That is why we wrote *Ideas Are Free*.

The book has its origins in the late 1980s when we both were on the faculty of the University of Massachusetts. Before going into academe, Dean Schroeder had headed a number of organizational turnarounds and major change initiatives, and had learned that the employees of distressed companies could often identify and solve critical problems which management had either missed or ignored. Invariably, they had penetrating insight into the issues that their companies faced and good ideas about how to address them. Why, Dean wondered, had their managers made no use of this free and willing resource?

Around this time, Alan Robinson came to ask the same question. He was studying how leading Japanese companies were managed. Many of them had higher productivity and better products than their Western counterparts, and he wanted to understand why. Through professional contacts and family members living and working in Japan, he was able to gain unusual access to twenty Japanese companies. Alan found that these companies put a great deal of emphasis on something that most Westerners had largely overlooked.

The Japanese managers were asking ordinary employees— the ones who staffed the offices, worked in the factories, and served the customers—for their ideas. *Small* ideas. Not creative whiz-bang new product or service ideas, but *everyday common-sense* ideas that would save a little money or time, make their jobs easier, improve the customer experience, or in some other way make the company better. Some of the companies Alan studied were getting and using extraordinary numbers of ideas—in some cases almost one per person per *week*. And these ideas accumulated into significant competitive advantage.

We both found the concept of seeking employee ideas compelling—it was clear how this would lead to high employee involvement and superior performance. Strangely, the vast majority of companies we were familiar with seemed to ignore this huge opportunity. Most of them were far better at *suppressing* ideas than *promoting* them.

The journey that led to *Ideas Are Free* began as a process of informal discovery. We gathered general information about how different organizations deal with employee ideas, visited some that did it well, and studied the history of efforts to promote employee ideas around the world. Ever since the Scottish shipbuilder William Denny put up the world's first industrial suggestion box in 1886, a wide variety of approaches to promoting employee ideas have been tried. Even Stalin tried to coax improvement ideas from front-line workers in the Soviet Union as part of his effort to catch up with the West.

We found that radical change did indeed take place when managers began encouraging and implementing large numbers of employee ideas. The implications were vast and profound—for improving performance, the organization's culture, and the quality of people's lives. Although few of the companies that were managing ideas well were publicizing their success, it was clear that the number of these companies was growing. And the deep transformation that these organizations experienced as ideas began to flow smoothly made us realize that we were looking at something quite revolutionary.

Our goal then was to figure out how organizations can successfully promote employee ideas and to understand the nature of the extreme change that pursuing ideas can create. The research turned out to be much more extensive than we anticipated. It took us to seventeen countries and into more than 150 organizations, representing a broad variety of industries—financial services, retailing, health care, manufacturing, hospitality, agriculture, publishing, high technology, transportation and logistics, telecommunications, not-for-profit, and government—and ranging in size from small family-owned businesses to large multinational corporations, in both union and nonunion environments. We studied best-practice companies and those whose attempts were struggling or just being launched. We compared what *worked* with what *didn't*, developed hypotheses, and tested them against our spectrum of organizations. We repeated the process until we were confident that we had distilled the general principles needed for success.

As people learned of our research, we found ourselves being invited to help many organizations that wanted to promote employee ideas. The hundreds of managers we worked with helped us further refine, clarify, and strengthen the concepts we now present in *Ideas Are Free*.

Tapping the potential in employee ideas is not a matter of merely buying into the concept and becoming more receptive and welcoming to them. There is a considerable amount to know, much of which is counterintuitive. We believe every manager should read this book, from the front-line supervisor to the CEO.

We hope that you enjoy *Ideas Are Free* and that it makes you a better leader.

ACKNOWLEDGMENTS

This book would not have come about without the help of a great many people.

First, we thank the many people in the organizations we studied who gave generously of their time and shared information openly with us. A few of them deserve special mention: at American Airlines, John Ford (business analyst) and Steven Groffman (senior financial analyst); at BIC Corporation, Linda Kwong (director, corporate communications), Philip Preston (employee involvement specialist), Charlie Tichy (employee involvement coordinator), and Ray Winter (former president and COO); Martin Edelston, CEO of Boardroom; at Dana, Gary Corrigan (vice president of corporate communications), Joe Magliochetti (the late CEO and chairman), and Ed Schultz (retired CEO of Dana Commercial Credit); at DUBAL, Shawqi Sajwani (manager, Environment, Health & Safety) and CEO John Boardman; at

Good Shepherd Services, Mary Ann Kehoe (managing director), Tom Lohuis (nursing home director), and Matt Gehri (business director); Eve Searle, CEO of Grapevine Canyon Ranch; Leslie Fishbein, president of Kacey Fine Furniture; at LaSalle Bank, JoAnne Tesmond (vice president and IdeaCenter coordinator) and Harrison Tempest (retired chairman); at Milliken, Tom Malone (president), Roger Milliken (CEO and chairman), and Craig Long (vice president, Milliken University and Quality); at Monrovia, Kim Marquardt (benefits manager) and Lupe Contreras (training manager); at Winnebago, Bruce Hertzke (CEO and chairman), Charles Tweeten (suggestion process administrator), and Cathy Stensland (suggestion process facilitator); and Don Wainwright, CEO and chairman of Wainwright Industries.

We also thank the many front-line employees—who do the work and come up with the ideas that are the subject of this book—for sharing their stories with us.

We owe a lot to our home institutions, the University of Massachusetts and Valparaiso University, which gave us the leeway and support needed to write this book. At the Isenberg School of Management at the University of Massachusetts, the staff was outstanding and made our work infinitely easier. Our heartfelt thanks go to Rebecca Jerome, Diane Kelley, Donna MacCartney, Courtney Spalding-Mayer, Mary Parker, Peter Sax, Nicole Tominsky, and Linda Vassalo. We are particularly grateful to Tom O'Brien, dean of the Isenberg School of Management, for his unwavering support and interest. Five of our former students also deserve mention: Louise Oestberg, Madhav Shriram, and Linda Randall, who were invaluable in setting up research visits to companies in Sweden, India, and the Soviet Union, respectively; and Jennifer Boulais and Kelly Druzisky, who helped with some of the research at Good Shepherd Services.

Valparaiso University provided funding support through the Herbert and Agnes Schulz Professorship. Erin Brown, MBA coordinator, was infinitely patient with her director and provided considerable moral support. MBA students Dru Bergman, Brad Scott, Susan Scroggins, Andrew Steele, and Doug Tougaw provided invaluable research assistance with Good Shepherd.

We are grateful to Isaac Getz, coauthor with Alan of *Vos Idées Changent Tout* (Paris: Éditions d'Organization, 2003) for kindly allowing us to use one of the stories from this French research project in *Ideas Are Free*.

Perhaps the hardest part of our journey was the writing of the manuscript, which went through many drafts as we struggled to articulate what our data were telling us. Gwen and J. Alan Robinson helped us immeasurably in this process, always asking probing questions and challenging us to simplify and clarify our ideas.

We would never have been able to produce this book without the invaluable advice of our editor Steve Piersanti and the rest of the incomparable staff at Berrett-Koehler.

Most important, we cannot begin to express what we owe our families, who lived every minute of the journey with us and cheerfully endured our lengthy and numerous absences. To our children Phoebe, Margot, Lexie, Liz, and Tori and particularly to our wives Margaret and Kate, we can only say: We could not have done it without you.

Alan Robinson   Dean Schroeder
Amherst, MA   *Valparaiso, IN*
January 2004   *January 2004*

CHAPTER 1

THE IDEA REVOLUTION

What will future generations say about the way we practice management today? What will they consider our most conspicuous failure?

We believe they will accuse us of having squandered one of the most significant resources available to us: employee ideas. Every day, all over the world, millions of working people see problems and opportunities that their managers do not. With little chance to do anything about them, they are forced to watch helplessly as their organizations waste money, disappoint and lose customers, and miss opportunity after opportunity that to them are all too apparent. The result is performance far lower than it should be and employees who do not respect or trust management and who are not fully engaged with their work.

At the same time, their managers are under constant pressure to do more with less. But with so much of their time consumed by "firefighting" and trying to meet short-term demands, they have little or no time to think about how to build their organizations' capabilities. They are chronically short of the resources they need to keep performance at current levels, much less *improve* it. They wonder how to motivate their employees, who don't seem as involved in their work as they should be. In short, a great many managers today find their work stressful and unfulfilling. Because there seems to be no alternative, both managers and employees become jaded, and they accept the situation as the way things have to be.

But a quiet revolution is under way—an *idea revolution*—led by managers and supervisors who, in a small but growing number of companies, have learned how to listen systematically to their employees. With each implemented idea, performance improves in some way. Some time or money is saved, someone's job becomes a little easier, the customer experience is enhanced, or the organization is improved in some other way. With large numbers of ideas coming in, performance improves *dramatically*. And as employees see their ideas used, they know they are having an impact on their organization and become engaged in their work.

Why do we call this movement a revolution? We do so because it liberates people and transforms the way that organizations are run. It changes the nature of the relationship between managers and their employees. As Ray Winter, then president of BIC Corporation, observed about the effect of his company's idea system on the corporate culture:

> *This system has taught my managers **real** respect for their employees. My managers have learned that their employees can make them look awfully good, if they only let them.*

This comment could easily be taken to mean that it does not take much—other than receptiveness on the part of management—to get large numbers of ideas from employees. But, just as it did the other companies we have studied, it took BIC years of experimentation and learning to discover how to tap this potential. There is a lot to learn, much of which goes against the initial assumptions most managers make about why people give ideas and which ideas are important.

—■————————

WHAT'S IN AN IDEA?

Ideas are the engine of progress. They improve people's lives by creating better ways to do things. They build and grow successful organizations and keep them healthy and prosperous. Without the ability to get new ideas, an organization stagnates and declines and eventually will be eliminated by competitors who *do* have fresh ideas.

An idea begins when a person becomes aware of a problem or opportunity, however small. Every day, regular employees— the people who do the office work, make the products, and serve the customers—see plenty of problems and opportunities and come up with good ideas about how to address them:

- When accounting for oil purchases, a staffer in a regional distribution center of Deutsche Post, the German post office, noticed that the company was paying too much for the engine oil for its trucks. Drivers were buying oil at roadside service stations, paying the equivalent of $8.50 per liter. After some research, he found that Deutsche Post could buy the oil in bulk for a quarter of the price and proposed that it do so. At the time of this writing, the idea was being implemented at distribution centers across Germany. With tens of thousands of diesel trucks and vans on the road, it will no doubt save millions of euros every year.

- At Good Shepherd Services, a not-for-profit health care organization with a nursing home in northern Wisconsin, a group of employees learned in a training session that dementia patients often see areas of black flooring as holes and avoid them. Instead of using alarm bracelets or restraints to keep such patients from wandering into unsafe areas, the group suggested simply to paint the floor black in front of the doorways to these areas. The idea worked, and it not only reduced patient stress but saved staff considerable time because they no longer had to respond to alarms.

- At LaSalle Bank, one of the largest banks in the United States, whenever someone requested a new laser printer, they were given the standard model specified by the purchasing department. One day, an employee unpacking his new printer noticed that it included an expensive internal disk drive, which no one would ever use. With all the printers the bank purchased each year, his idea to eliminate this feature saved a considerable sum of money.

- At a Massachusetts Department of Correction facility, a guard proposed a change in the way pictures were taken of new inmates. Instead of using film, why not use digital cameras and store the images in a database? Across the department's sixteen correctional facilities, this idea saved $56,000 the first year in film alone.

- An office worker in a Florida branch of a national temporary-placement firm realized that there was a problem with her company's screening practices. At the time, it was paying an outside vendor to test applicants for literacy, numeracy, and computer skills. Those who passed were then given a drug test and criminal background check, which some *70 percent* failed. Why not do the drug testing and criminal background check *first*, she asked? When the idea was implemented nationwide, the savings were huge.

- At Winnebago Industries, the recreational vehicle maker, an assembly worker pointed out that the 10 percent of customers who ordered the deluxe sound system option were getting additional speakers they never used. No one had told the crews on the main assembly line that installed the built-in speakers for the *regular* sound systems to skip the vehicles that would be having the deluxe speakers installed later. The regular speakers embedded in the walls were never connected. They were *seen* but not heard. Although the savings from this idea were significant, the main benefit was that customers stopped bringing vehicles back to the dealers and asking them to fix speakers that were not working.

None of these ideas required particular insight or much creativity, or required much in the way of time or resources to implement. (In the case of Deutsche Post, oil suppliers were so eager for the business, they were willing to install the bulk tanks for free.) To the people who came up with them, they were simply common sense.

Every employee idea, no matter how small, improves an organization in some way. It is when managers are able to get *large numbers* of such ideas that the full power of the idea revolution is unleashed.

as Management respect goes up so do the ideas

────────■────────

HOW IDEAS DRIVE A CULTURE OF HIGH PERFORMANCE

There is a clear link between an organization's ability to tap ideas and its overall performance. Consider the following examples:

- Boardroom Inc., a Connecticut publisher, averaged 104 ideas per employee in 2002. Its sales per employee were more than seven times greater than the average publisher.

- Richer Sounds has been listed a number of times in the *Guinness Book of World Records* as having the highest sales per square foot of any retailer in the world. It also has one of the best idea systems in the United Kingdom, which brings in some twenty ideas per employee per year.

- Milliken, a global fabric and specialty chemicals company, averaged 110 ideas per employee in 2002. In a number of its textile product lines, it competes with companies in developing nations whose prevailing wages are less than *one-twentieth* of those in Europe and the United States, where most Milliken operations are located. To be successful, the company has to *outmanage* these competitors. Over the last two decades, Milliken has actually been able to *increase* its advantage over them, a feat that Roger Milliken, chairman and CEO, attributes in large part to the company's idea system. Milliken is one of only two companies in the world that has won both the Malcolm Baldrige National Quality Award (MBNQA) and the European Quality Award. The other is the French-Italian company ST Microelectronics, which has one of the better idea systems in Europe.

- DUBAL, a major aluminum company in the United Arab Emirates, has none of the natural advantages typically associated with aluminum producers. It must produce its own electricity, desalinate seawater from the Persian Gulf to get the large amount of fresh water it needs, and import its primary raw materials from Australia. Yet DUBAL, whose people average more than nine ideas each per year, is one of the lowest-cost producers of aluminum in the world. According to CEO John Boardman, much of the company's excellent performance can be credited to its idea system.

- Dana Corporation, a global company with over sixty thousand people, expects every employee to submit two ideas each month, and in some facilities it exceeds twice this number, with a worldwide implementation rate of *80 percent.* Two of the company's U.S. divisions have won the MBNQA.

In our experience, when people first encounter examples of companies like these—work environments that are clearly so different from where *they* work—they are full of questions. How do the employees in these organizations come up with so many ideas? Are the ideas any good? Who has time to deal with all of them? Don't you have to create a huge bureaucracy just to deal with ideas? How are employees motivated to give in so many ideas? Are they offered rewards? These are all good questions, and we will answer them in this book. But before we do, it is important to understand just how radical the concept of going after large numbers of employee ideas is. It brings about so much change, in fact, that for most managers it is revolutionary.

Ever since Frederick Taylor first advocated that management's job was to *think* and the worker's job to *do*, this has been the default perspective. In most organizations around the world, the division between thinking and doing is "hard-wired" into policies, structures, and operating practices, although it is rarely explicit or even recognized for what it is. While this approach may have been the right one a hundred years ago, today it has become severely limiting. This is why the simple concept of going after employee ideas—when done properly—fundamentally transforms the way organizations are run, allows them to achieve levels of performance well beyond what they were previously capable of, and liberates the people working in them.

The mechanics alone of handling large quantities of ideas *forces* considerable change. Managers whose employees are submitting one or two ideas *every week* cannot hope to evaluate, test, and implement them all unless they push decision-making authority for most of them back down closer to the employees and their supervisors. This empowerment starts a virtuous cycle. As employees see their ideas being used, they begin to feel valued as part of the team and become more involved. As managers see this change in attitude and the impact that ideas have on performance, their respect for employees grows. Employees are trusted with more information, training, and authority. This in turn leads to even more and better ideas—and the cycle continues, ultimately creating a positive, high-performance culture.

THE NEED FOR MANAGERIAL HUMILITY

It is easy for managers and supervisors to come to believe that they know better than the people who work for them. After all, they are usually better educated, have merited positions of greater responsibility, and earn significantly more money. They wear the "suits." Managers who get large numbers of ideas from their employees have the opposite view. In our experience, they are much less arrogant. They recognize their heavy dependence on input from their subordinates. Every day, they are reminded of how valuable front-line ideas can be.

In a famous essay, Friedrich Hayek, founder of the Austrian School of Economics, articulated why employees often see problems and opportunities that their managers do not.[1] In writing about decision making in organizations, Hayek divided knowledge into two types: *aggregate* knowledge and knowledge *of the particular circumstances of time and place*. Managers usually deal with the first kind of knowledge—things like "Sales are off 10 percent" or "Costs went up 5 percent." The higher a person is in an organization, the more aggregated his or her information tends to be. While aggregate knowledge is important for understanding general relationships and formulating broad strategies, it is not very useful for coming up with specific performance-improving ideas. These come primarily from the second kind of knowledge that Hayek discussed—the detailed knowledge of particular events, day-to-day problems and opportunities, and how things are actually done. This is exactly what employees tend to possess and why they can often come up with better ways to meet organizational goals than their managers can.

We came across a particularly telling instance of this fact when we helped set up an idea system for one of the world's largest cranberry growers, a company with more than forty-five thousand acres of bogs under cultivation. At a time when cranberry prices were plummeting, management was desperate for ideas that could save money, other than ones involving more layoffs. The value of being on the spot showed in one of the very first ideas that came in. Cranberry production, like rice production, is water-intensive, and pumping large volumes of water is extremely costly. The idea, which came from a field worker, was simple: "When it rains, turn off the sprinkler systems."

---■---

WHY ORGANIZATIONS NEVER RUN OUT OF IMPROVEMENT OPPORTUNITIES

Two questions managers often ask when they learn how well some companies are doing at getting employee ideas are "Don't employees ever run out of ideas?" and "Can an organization get so good that there is nothing left to improve?"

If these were real concerns, one company that would have had to deal with them is Toyota. In 1992, Yuzo Yasuda published a book about the company's idea system, entitled *40 Years, 20 Million Ideas*. It told how Toyota got more than a million ideas per year from its employees and had been doing so for more than a decade. Around this time, a U.S. Army lieutenant general asked one of us how this could be. To him, it made no sense. Either Toyota was in very bad shape, he asserted—so bad that it needed a million ideas per year to fix its problems—or the whole thing was some kind of charade. Whichever was the case,

Toyota's idea system didn't seem to be something other companies would want to emulate. It was a thoughtful comment from someone with considerable leadership experience. But it also exposed a degree of ignorance.

Let us look at the two possible explanations the general proposed. First, Toyota is hardly a screwed-up organization. In fact, it is one of the most successful automakers, and one of the most admired companies, in the world. And as for the idea system being some kind of charade, it is instead absolutely *central* to Toyota's management philosophy. Toyota has long been a relentless improver. As Yasuda's book pointed out, ever since 1951, a top executive—including several future CEOs and chairmen, and even members of the founding Toyoda family—has headed the company's idea system. What is more, many members of its board of directors have been personally involved in idea system activities. Few companies have ever matched this level of top management commitment to listening to employee suggestions. A significant percentage of the company's overall improvement comes from its idea system.

As for the quantity of ideas being a sign of a company with an inordinate number of problems, perhaps the general would be correct if the world never changed. Sooner or later, Toyota might get everything right and employees would run out of ideas. But everything changes, and changes constantly: technologies, competitors, customers, suppliers, employees, the economy, the overall business environment—*everything*. To stay competitive, a company has to respond. And since an organization is a living, interconnected, and integrated system, an action taken in one place influences things elsewhere. In other words, change creates the need for further change. New problems and opportunities are born all the time. There will never be a shortage of them, and the faster an organization can spot and act on them, the more successful it will be.

■

OVERVIEW OF THE BOOK'S MAIN POINTS

This book is organized into eight chapters. Chapters 2 and 3 deal with two fundamental principles of managing ideas that are highly counterintuitive—the importance of going after small ideas rather than big ones, and the problems with the most common reward schemes and how to avoid them. Chapters 4 and 5 describe how to make ideas part of everyone's job, and how to set up and run an effective process for handling ideas. Chapters 6 and 7 show how to take a good idea system and make it *great*, by focusing employee ideas on the areas where they are most needed and by helping employees come up with more and better ideas. Chapter 8, the final chapter, shows how good idea systems have a profound impact on an organization's culture. At the end of each chapter (except this one and chapter 8), we provide "Guerrilla Tactics"—actions to promote ideas that any manager can take on his or her own authority and that require little or no resources.

The remainder of this chapter provides a brief overview of the main points in the book.

The Importance of Small Ideas

In 2001, we were asked to help a German automobile manufacturer beef up its idea system. "It is so hard in our business today," its managers told us. "We figure out a way to cut significant costs out of our operation, and before we are finished, we have to start looking for the next big cost-cutting idea. We never seem to be able to relax or get any breathing space. Every one of us works long hours and is exhausted all the time."

These managers couldn't seem to create much advantage that was *sustainable*—most major improvement initiatives undertaken were quickly countered by other automakers, and any advantage gained from them soon evaporated. The root cause of the problem, we soon realized, was that these managers thought that big ideas were the only way to get ahead.

Business leaders are always looking for the next breakthrough idea—the "home run" that will put them well ahead of the competition with one swing. Because of this, the systems and policies they put in place are aimed at *big* ideas. Few managers realize how severely limiting this is. In chapter 2, we explain why it is much smarter to go after the *small* ideas.

For one thing, as that German auto manufacturer had already discovered, the bigger an idea the more likely it is that competitors will discover and counter it. If it affects the company's products or services, it is directly visible—in fact, it may well be *advertised.* If the idea involves a major process change behind the scenes, it is often copied even more rapidly. Significant internal initiatives usually require outside suppliers, contractors, or consultants—people whose jobs are to sell their products, services, and expertise. And companies are proud of their latest innovations. They like to impress their customers with them. These same customers might well share the exciting new development with their other suppliers. No matter how hard the managers in that German company worked to get big cost-cutting ideas, they were unlikely to develop much sustainable competitive advantage from them. While the big ideas were necessary to keep up with the competition, they were not sufficient to get ahead and stay there.

Small ideas, on the other hand, are much less likely to migrate to competitors. They are often site- and situation-specific, and therefore of little use outside the company anyway. For example, when the *Vidette Times*, a regional newspaper in Indiana, ran out of newsprint late one night owing to a strike at its Canadian supplier, the press operator was ready with a backup plan—not a great one, but one the company could limp along with. Although his presses used rolls that were forty-five inches in diameter, earlier that day he had borrowed some *forty-seven-inch* rolls from a sister operation, just in case. His plan was that if the new shipment of forty-five-inch rolls didn't arrive in time, he and his coworker would manually unroll the larger rolls until they fit on the *Vidette Times*' printing press. They were not looking forward to this, as it would involve stripping *thousands* of feet of paper off rolls that weighed more than three tons.

When the shipment of forty-five-inch rolls didn't turn up, the two men brought a forty-seven-inch roll across to the press on their forklift truck, to see exactly how much they would have to unwind in order to squeeze it on. To their astonishment, they found that it just fit as it was. The press manufacturer's specification had been too conservative. Their discovery had significant implications. Being able to use larger rolls of paper saved the company thousands of dollars per year, because it meant fewer roll changes, and hundreds of fewer "trial copies" needed to get the ink flowing again after each roll change. It also shaved about a half-hour per night off the press run.

The point is this: When this idea came up, the *Vidette Times* was in the middle of a circulation war. Had it come up with an innovative new column or marketing approach, its archrival would have been aware of it immediately. But how would it learn about the forty-seven-inch roll idea? And even if it had, it wouldn't have mattered, since the competitor didn't have the same model of printing press. Because most small ideas remain proprietary in this way, they accumulate into a tremendous competitive advantage that is *sustainable*, the kind of advantage managers *should* be striving for. Ironically, what would have really relieved the pressure on the managers at that German automaker was the very thing they had all but issued direct orders to ignore.

Small ideas also enable an organization to pay exceptional attention to detail. In many important aspects of business— such as customer service, responsiveness, quality, and managing costs—excellence means getting the details right. It is simply impossible to improve performance beyond a certain level without small ideas. And a superior ability to handle details, in turn, raises the level of complexity an organization can deal with effectively. This can allow an organization to do things its competitors literally *cannot do.*

Perhaps the ultimate irony is that managing small ideas is the most effective way to get big ones, a phenomenon we shall also describe in chapter 2, along with several other surprising benefits of small ideas.

If small ideas are the goal, the challenge becomes one of designing a cost-effective process to evaluate and implement them. That is the subject we turn to next.

The Problems with Rewards

Whenever managers start to think about how to promote ideas, the question of rewards almost always pops up. In the late 1990s, the British government released a white paper entitled

"Modernizing Government," in which Prime Minister Tony Blair and his cabinet laid out a comprehensive and long-term plan for reforming the way the government worked. One of its key initiatives was to make the Civil Service more innovative, by giving employees an "incentive to change behavior":

> *We will foster innovation and continuous improvement of services in the public sector by rewarding staff who suggest ideas that lead to savings or better services. Government Departments and agencies will introduce schemes which reward staff with a sliding scale percentage of any savings or improvements made as a result of their suggestions.*[2]

On the surface, offering rewards for ideas commensurate with their value seems a smart thing to do. The more generous the rewards, the more ideas will come in. So the thinking goes. The British government is far from alone in this regard. It is an easy conceptual trap to fall into. A great many managers have unwittingly sabotaged their efforts to promote employee ideas by making exactly the same mistake. The problem is not in sharing the benefits of ideas with employees—this can be done very effectively—but in doing so with rewards for individual ideas based on their value.

Consider this: Not one of the companies we mentioned earlier that has been successful at getting large numbers of ideas from its employees offers rewards in this way. As we shall explain in chapter 3, not only do such rewards substantially increase the cost, time, and effort needed to evaluate and implement ideas, but they create a host of unanticipated problems that end up acting as *disincentives* for people to offer ideas. It is ironic that so many managers have such faith in a motivational tool that actually works *against* them.

The first set of problems has to do with calculating the value of an idea. It can be very time-consuming to quantify the effect of even the simplest idea. Take, for example, the first idea mentioned in this chapter—the one at Deutsche Post to buy oil in bulk for one-fourth of the cost. Deutsche Post gives employees 10 percent of the annual value of their ideas. In this case, calculating the reward seems simple enough. But someone has to spend the time figuring out how much oil Deutsche Post uses, because the company does not track it centrally. Furthermore, not only does Deutsche Post have some eighty-three distribution centers, but it may take years to implement the idea at all of them. Some of the centers are even *resisting* the idea, because they have to go through the hassle of installing the tanks and getting special environmental licenses and inspections. These costs, too, have to be factored into the reward. And, of course, the price of oil fluctuates, and even varies by region within Germany. What price should the company pick to make the calculations? From the point of view of estimating cost savings, *most* ideas are more complicated than this one. Having to determine the worth of every single idea means a tremendous amount of non-value-adding work. And since it is impossible to calculate the value of most ideas accurately anyway, whatever numbers are produced are often perceived as underestimates by the very people the rewards are intended to thank and motivate. In the 1980s, United Airlines abolished its suggestion system—one of the oldest in the United States at the time—because of the large number of disputes that arose in this way.

In his classic essay "On the Folly of Rewarding A, While Hoping for B," Steven Kerr articulates another set of problems with rewards. Often, rewards that are intended to promote desirable behaviors are actually encouraging undesirable behaviors. And when it comes to rewards based on the value of ideas, the list of detrimental side effects is long. For example, rewards are usually given only to the *originator* of the idea. Doing anything else would be incredibly complicated. But this undermines the teamwork necessary to bring off most ideas. The contributions of the people involved in evaluating, testing, and implementing them are largely ignored, and they often resent it. Why should they put in extra work to develop an idea, when *someone else* will collect the reward for it? The most common complaint we hear from idea system managers in companies that use rewards is that it is hard to get anyone to evaluate and implement ideas. And when they can persuade someone to look at an idea, the easiest course of action for that person to take is to find a reason to *reject* it.

A poorly designed reward scheme can also interfere with the free flow of ideas in more nefarious ways. It can give rise to unethical behavior, as managers look for ways to save money on rewards they owe, and workers look to "game" the system for higher payouts. When potentially large sums of money are at stake, managers and employees can be tempted into outright fraud and corruption. As the saying goes, "If money can be made by doing something wrong, someone will." For organizations that use such reward schemes, unethical behavior can turn into a real problem.

But as we shall also explain in chapter 3, perhaps the most surprising aspect of rewards, and the good news for managers concerned about the issues they raise, is that they really are not needed. People give in ideas because they *want* to see them used. Either they see a way to make their jobs easier or less frustrating, or they find an opportunity to improve the organization in some way. Employees also have a natural pride in their work; they like to feel valued and to know they are having an impact. As the experience of many companies shows—including several whose idea systems could be considered among the best in the world—employees willingly give in large numbers of ideas without the prospect of monetary rewards. The most important rewards they get are seeing their ideas used and being recognized for them.

This does not mean that organizations should avoid rewarding their people with substantial money for their ideas. Rewards *can* be given, provided they are properly structured. A number of companies with high-performing idea systems—including several we have already mentioned, such as Boardroom, Wainwright, and Dana—give substantial rewards for ideas. On average, employees in these companies get far more money from their ideas than they would earn under traditional schemes.

Making Ideas a Central Part of Work

In 1997, we took a busload of college students on a study trip to Canada. One of the visits was to a large subsidiary of a well-known U.S. company. After a tour of the facility, the company assembled a panel of its senior managers for a question-and-answer session. At one point, the discussion turned to the suggestion system. When a student asked how many ideas the company was getting from its roughly two thousand employees, the conversation took an interesting turn.

"Last year, I think it was three," the general manager replied.

"Was that three per employee or three *in total?*" the question came back.

"Oh, three total." And then, quite unabashedly, the manager turned to his management team and remarked, "Come to think of it, I still have some ideas on my desk from the late 1980s that I probably should do something about."

On paper, this company had a process for seeking and acting on employee ideas. But with the lack of management interest and follow-through, it might as well not have bothered. It was getting an average of one idea per employee every *six hundred years.*

The general manager's comment is jarring because it reveals a complete lack of concern for something that should have been extremely important to him. Had he worked at a company that valued ideas, his casual remark would have been as outrageous as his announcing publicly, "I still have some financial reports to finish from the late 1980s that I must get to sometime."

Any system, no matter how well conceived, works only if people are held accountable for the roles they have to play. In chapter 4, we describe how to put accountability into the process of managing ideas at all levels in the organization.

Organizations that are successful at getting ideas monitor which employees are turning them in, which managers are getting them, and how rapidly they are acted on. Employees and managers are given appropriate training and support, and then held accountable for their roles in the idea process. Coming up with ideas is made a central part of the employees' work. Supervisors and middle managers are assessed on how well they do at *promoting* ideas. The supervisor's role is to coach, mentor, and encourage employees and to champion ideas with broader implications. Middle managers need to ensure that ideas are processed rapidly and fairly and that appropriate resources are available for implementation. They often must get directly involved with ideas whose impact is more significant or cross-functional.

Finally, in addition to their oversight responsibilities, top managers should have roles that routinely bring them into direct contact with suggesters and their ideas. This not only shows that top managers support employee ideas, but it keeps them in closer touch with what is happening in the trenches. There is a huge difference between the actions of a leader who sees employees as a tremendous source of improvement ideas and one who sees them as a *cost* to be minimized.

Making Change Easy

Visualize your organization's suggestion box, stuffed with ideas. If you were responsible for processing these ideas, would you be excited to open the box or horrified at the prospect?

Managers at a Fortune 100 company with a traditional suggestion system told us that it cost approximately $500 and took four hours of staff and management time to process each idea— just to *process* it, not to implement it. Suppose that Milliken, whose 16,000 employees average 110 ideas each per year, had such a cumbersome and expensive process! The resulting overhead would be crippling: $880 million, or $55,000 per employee, and over 7 million labor hours, the equivalent of 3,600 full-time employees, more than *20 percent* of its current workforce. If Milliken had an idea process like that Fortune 100 company, it could not afford to ask its employees to think on the job.

To be able to handle large numbers of ideas in a cost-effective way, an organization has to drastically reduce the time and effort needed to evaluate and implement them. While the specific processes employed can vary greatly between companies, every effective approach we know of follows the same basic principles.

Take the process at Boardroom Inc., for example. Each week, every employee is expected to come up with two ideas—no matter how small—and bring them to his or her departmental meeting. During the meeting, everyone (including the manager) presents his or her ideas in turn. After each one is explained, the group discusses it and, if possible, improves on it. If members of the group decide that the idea can be used, they determine who will be responsible for implementation (usually the person who came up with it). If the proposal needs further consideration or review at a higher level, someone will be assigned to follow through. The average meeting involves eight to ten people, lasts forty-five minutes, and, in addition to taking care of normal departmental business, processes some twenty ideas.

Boardroom's deceptively simple process—which has evolved significantly since it was started in the early 1990s, when *every* idea went to the CEO—has most of the attributes of an effective system.[3] First, ideas are part of everyone's normal work. Second, it is easy to submit ideas. Third, ideas are reviewed and discussed by people who have direct knowledge of the situation at hand, who will be directly affected if the idea is implemented and who can build on or help modify it so that it will work better. Fourth, decision making is rapid, effective, and efficient. Fifth, feedback to the suggester is quick and complete—in this case because he or she is present in the room. Sixth, whenever possible, ideas are implemented almost immediately, often before higher-level managers even become aware of them. Finally, the system itself is actively managed and constantly improved.

Like all good idea systems, Boardroom's is highly attuned to the way the company operates, to its culture, and to its particular needs and goals. What is important here is not *how* the company addresses each of the attributes of a good idea system described here but that it *does* address them, and does so effectively. In chapter 5, we discuss these attributes in more detail and describe some of the different ways companies have incorporated them into the way they operate.

Drawing Attention to What Is Important

In the early 1990s, Winnebago Industries had a sales opportunity it did not want to lose. Demand for high-margin options, such as microwave ovens and generators, on its popular Micro-Mini models was strong, but the company could not meet it. Unfortunately, the Micro-Mini was close to its vehicle weight limit, a limit that Winnebago is always very careful to stay below. To be able to offer customers the options they might want, its weight had to be reduced.

By writing an open letter in the company's newspaper, *The Smoke Signal*, and by a variety of other means, chairman and founder John K. Hanson let his employees know about the opportunity and asked them for ideas, however small, that would reduce the weight of the vehicle. Within a month he had received more than two hundred—many of them for just a few ounces—that collectively solved the problem. Here are some examples:

- Remove the two heavy metal hooks that the Japanese supplier bolted to the bottom of each chassis so that it could be chained down on the ships during its journey across the Pacific.

- Stop installing special steel brackets into the walls of the vehicles' master bedrooms, since the mirrors they were designed to hold have been replaced with lightweight murals.

- Stop installing carpeting under the beds, since they are bolted flush to the floor anyway.

By drawing attention to the opportunity the company faced, Hanson made weight-saving ideas legitimate. Before, the weight of the vehicles was primarily the responsibility of the engineers. Front-line employees were not concerned about it, and even if they had come up with ideas to reduce weight, their managers might not have taken these ideas seriously. But once Hanson alerted the entire organization to the issue, his front-line people came up with plenty of weight-saving ideas, and these were quickly implemented. With relatively little additional effort, he had given his idea system a target and turned it into a powerful competitive weapon.

In chapter 6 we discuss how managers go about focusing employee ideas on critical areas. These range from initiatives to take advantage of specific one-time opportunities like that of Winnebago, to ongoing practices that keep everyone focused on the key strategic drivers of performance.

Helping Employees See Beyond the Obvious

In the mid-1990s, one of the world's largest airlines spent millions of dollars putting its employees through creativity training. Looking back on the effort a few years later, the executive in charge of the initiative remarked to one of us that all it had really accomplished was to create a lot of frustration. When the training was over, the participants returned to their jobs expecting their company to be open to their ideas. Unfortunately, the company had not changed while they were away, and it remained just as unresponsive to them as it had always been. The real bottleneck to creativity all along—this lack of responsiveness to ideas—had not been addressed.

Once an organization has an effective idea system in place, however, it makes sense to do what this airline did and begin to think about ways to increase the quantity and quality of the ideas people come up with. In chapter 7, we describe proven approaches to doing this. The key point is this: Any approach must build on the ways that people *already* come up with ideas at work. Too often, this seemingly obvious point is overlooked.

People think of ideas because they see a better way of doing something, or an opportunity to exploit. To have a good idea requires a combination of perspective, knowledge, and alertness. In chapter 7, we describe what we have come to call "idea activators"—training sessions aimed at helping participants see more improvement opportunities in important areas. We use examples from Toyota and Good Shepherd Services to show how different organizations have developed their idea activators to produce impressive results. The chapter then turns to more general tactics that companies can use to broaden employees' perspectives and expose them to new ways of thinking. These tactics help them in different ways to spot considerably more problems and opportunities.

Profound Change

In the late 1980s, Wainwright Industries was becoming increasingly concerned about its future. The company operated in two very competitive industries—aerospace and automotive. Although sales were increasing, profit margins remained meager. Wainwright had tried to implement total quality management, but with mixed results. The company was not a happy place to work. As Mike Simms, its general manager, put it, as management retrenched, its tactics became increasingly based on fear, mistrust, and intimidation. Some of the company's middle managers were so frustrated that they had secretly met a number of times to discuss a leveraged buyout.

But then something happened that changed everything. In January 1991, a vice president from IBM-Rochester, which had just won the Malcolm Baldrige National Quality Award, came to speak at a local business breakfast meeting. A group of Wainwright managers were at the meeting, sitting at a table in the back. Simms, who did not particularly want to be there, was doodling on his napkin, when he heard the speaker say the words "sincere trust and belief in people." He looked up.

He wrote these words on his napkin and underneath them wrote, "What is that?" He passed the napkin to the person sitting next to him, who happened to be the company's comptroller.

She wrote, "I don't know what trust is. Do we have it at Wainwright?"

Simms wrote back, "If we don't know what trust in people is, we can't possibly have it." He passed it back to the comptroller and went back to his doodling. Without thinking, she passed the napkin on. A few minutes later, Mike Simms realized to his horror that the napkin had gone to CEO Don Wainwright and both other owners of the company. As the management team looked back to that event, there was general agreement that this had been a key moment for the company. It was when they collectively articulated what they had been missing all along. It was not that the *employees* didn't trust management, they all agreed; it was that *managers* didn't trust employees. And this, the management team realized, was holding the company back.

Trusting employees was the starting point for the company's effort to transform itself. Don Wainwright and the rest of the management team asked themselves a simple question: "If we *really* trusted our employees, how would we behave, and what would the benefits be?" The answer to this question was "We would listen to them and give them more ability to change things when they see a better way to do them." The transformation didn't happen immediately, but by staying true to the vision of increasing trust, gradually the TQM initiative began showing results. By 1994, performance had improved so much that the company won the Malcolm Baldrige National Quality Award. In presenting the award, Vice President Al Gore cited the company's world-class idea system as one of its most impressive achievements. Since that time, Wainwright has continued to improve and refine it. As mentioned earlier, in 2002, it averaged sixty-five implemented ideas per employee. It would be impossible for the company to handle all these ideas, unless it really did trust the employees to make good decisions and act on them.

In chapter 8, we discuss the connection between an organization's culture and its idea system. The culture of a company has always been, and will always be, very important for its success. Yet because it is so intangible, organizations find it difficult to measure and manage. However, organizations that successfully promote ideas have found that the performance of their idea systems is directly related to important aspects of their cultures—such as trust, respect, morale, involvement, and teamwork. They discovered that when employees see that their thinking is valued, attitudes change, and the corporate culture improves. This has a profound effect on performance and on the quality of the lives of everyone in the organization.

CONCLUSION

The world is becoming an increasingly competitive place. Those managers who recognize the potential in employee ideas and are able to encourage and use them, will be the ones who thrive. They will be able to create more pleasant and rewarding work environments, attract and retain better employees, and deliver superior performance. We believe future generations of managers will look back on us as having missed a huge opportunity. Managers who pay little attention to employee ideas will be viewed as having mismanaged a critical resource and as having paid a high price for it. The level of success with employee ideas will become a primary measure of the quality of a leader.

Don Wainwright once remarked to us that most business leaders manage from financial measures—that is, *lagging* indicators that impart mostly historical information. On the other hand, the most important indicator he uses is the number of ideas implemented in the previous week. This, he has learned, is the best *leading* indicator of his company's future performance. If he gets this number right, a great deal else will follow. Referring to the general tendency to manage predominantly by financial indicators, he told us that he could beat Pete Sampras or Patrick Rafter at tennis, if they watched the scoreboard while he watched the ball.

When managers first realize the value in the ideas of their employees, it is a profoundly liberating experience. When they learn how to go after these ideas, they also learn that it is well worth the time and effort. Ideas *are* free. Employees become allies in solving problems, spotting opportunities, and moving the company forward, to the benefit of all. And when managers decide to let their employees think alongside them—and no longer seek to go it alone—they will have joined the Idea Revolution.

CHAPTER 2

THE POWER OF SMALL IDEAS

Several years ago, one of us was invited to give a talk about managing ideas to a group of CEOs. Early on, when talking about small ideas, he was brusquely interrupted by one of them, the head of one of the largest producers of computer equipment in the United States.

"I think I speak for all of us when I ask you to please move on to talk about what we should do to get the blockbuster innovations, the ones that change the terms of competition in our industries. That's what we're really interested in."

Everyone is attracted by big and dramatic ideas. The more novel they are or the more far-reaching their implications, the more we are drawn to them. It is not surprising that managers (like that CEO), when thinking about employee ideas, envision the "home runs"—the suggestions generating hundreds of thousands or even millions of dollars or the breakthrough innovations that will propel their organizations to industry dominance. To them, the *currency* of managing ideas—that is, the unit to keep score with—is the big idea. In this chapter, we explain why managers should be paying more attention to the *small* ideas.

Most problems and opportunities that employees spot will be relatively small, so most of their ideas will be small, too. Managers who see little value in these ideas cut themselves off from most of the potential benefits of employee ideas. The irony is that in many ways small ideas are *more* valuable than big ones. Also, going after small ideas is the best way to get big ideas.

■

EXCELLENCE DEPENDS ON SMALL IDEAS

In the last chapter, we explained why managers do not see all the problems and opportunities that their employees do. This being the case, there is a limit to the results that can be obtained through top-down management. It is simply impossible to achieve excellence in many aspects of performance without the ability to pay attention to detail, an ability that comes only from large numbers of small ideas.

Customer Service

Grapevine Canyon Ranch is a resort in the high desert of southeastern Arizona, an area full of history. Tombstone is less than thirty miles away, and the ranch itself looks out over the former homelands of the great Apache chiefs Cochise and Geronimo. Guests come to Grapevine to enjoy the unspoiled beauty of this historic desert. The resort attracts discriminating customers from all over the world who want an authentic experience but who also expect relaxed, unobtrusive, and high-quality service. And this they get, because Grapevine has cultivated an extraordinary level of attention to detail through employee ideas.

Every two weeks, owner Eve Searle has a meeting with her employees, each of whom is expected to come with an idea that will improve some aspect of the ranch's operations. Table 2.1 shows a sampling of them. Notice the level of detail in these ideas, how they make the ranch more relaxed and efficient, and how they allow it to pick up on fine points and add nice touches.

Many of the ideas not only improve the guest experience but also make it easier for employees to get their jobs done. Take Sylvia's suggestion: "In the accommodations with showers, have maintenance glue a block on top of the shower head so the soap caddy stops falling to the floor." When this was implemented, not only did falling soap caddies no longer inconvenience the guests, but Sylvia no longer had to contend with the resulting messes. Rob's idea—"Put a cigarette butt receptacle by the swing"—is another instance. Not only does he no longer have to pick up the butts, allowing him time to do more value-adding things, but this change makes the swing area nicer for children and parents.

Or take Maria's idea: "Change the directions we give in our brochures to guests arriving from Ironwood." Many resorts would not pick up on poor directions so easily. Complaints from weary and frustrated travelers about bad standard-issue directions are typically made to front-desk clerks who can do little about them. But at Grapevine, as soon as one guest complained, it triggered an idea to change the directions, and this was done the following week.

Table 2.1. Examples of ideas from Grapevine Canyon Ranch

Who	Idea	Do It!!
Diane	Put directions and labels on the circuit breakers in the Cookshack.	Danny
Sylvia	Offer alcohol-free sparkling cider for nondrinkers on anniversaries.	Norma—do it!
Annie	Put a peg board in the barn with areas for Grapevine, CL, and other pastures. Use pegs or other markers to denote where horses are.	Good idea! Kitty?
Harald	I can translate ride and brochure information into German.	Great! Do it— Bonnie please give him all papers.
Ginger	Offer fruit in season dish as a dessert alternative (e.g., melon pieces on the lunch buffet).	Done!!
Rob	Put a cigarette butt receptacle by the swing.	Done!
Ross	Put a "kick-plate" on the door from the staff room into the kitchen so people can open it with their feet.	Do it! Danny
Bonnie	See if any of the magazines we advertise with have a Web site and can we link to it.	
Norma	Put a screen door on the west kitchen door to save on cooler costs.	Danny
Ross	Set up croquet or horseshoes by the oaks.	Do it!
Maria	Change the directions we give in our brochures to guests arriving from Ironwood.	Have to change all brochures.
Danny	Spray-paint water faucets—red for yard water, green for drinkable water.	Good idea! Do it.
Maria	Have a bacon sandwich for lunch on all day rides—won't spoil like lunch meat.	
Sylvia	In the accommodations with showers, have maintenance glue a block on top of the shower head so the soap caddy stops falling to the floor.	Good idea—Adam
Diane	The 15 mph sign needs to be placed one more pole to the south. As of now there is a mesquite bush and you don't see it.	Adam
Maria	Put a step stool in the tour van for the guests.	Done!

With practice, employees develop sharp observational skills. Take, for example, an idea that came from a housekeeper. From faint imprints left on the stacks of stationery in the rooms, she had realized that many guests were using full sheets of it—the only writing paper provided—to swap names and addresses with other guests. Using stationery for such a purpose was both inconvenient for the guests and costly, the housekeeper thought. Why not create special business-card-size pieces of paper with spaces for names, addresses, telephone numbers, and e-mail addresses? Today, each room has a small holder with these wallet-sized cards in it. They are convenient and remind guests of their stay at the ranch. How many hotels would have housekeeping staff this alert for improvement opportunities?

It is simply impossible to achieve excellence in performance without the ability to pay attention to detail, an ability that comes only from large numbers of small ideas.

All of the small ideas Grapevine Canyon Ranch gets from its employees accumulate over time and allow it to attain exceptionally high levels of productivity and customer satisfaction. The extraordinary attention to detail makes the service relaxed, courteous, and efficient. And the high levels of customer satisfaction mean that Grapevine can depend on a large percentage of repeat business and strong word-of-mouth advertising, allowing it to keep its marketing budget low and to attract customers whose expectations closely match the rustic experience it offers.

Responsiveness and Cycle Time

Responsiveness is another aspect of performance in which it is impossible to attain excellence without large numbers of small ideas. Perhaps the fact that most organizations do *not* actively seek small ideas explains the startling statistic that George Stalk and Thomas Hout document in their book *Competing against Time*: "Most products and many services are actually receiving value for only .05% to 5% of the time they are in the value delivery system of their companies."[1] In other words, 95 percent or more of the time, a product or service is simply waiting. Nothing is happening to it.

Over the last decade, interest in reducing cycle times has grown considerably. The ability to move faster than competitors is a powerful advantage. Again according to the authors of *Competing against Time*:

> *For every quartering of the time interval required to provide a service or product, the productivity of labor and of working capital can often double. These productivity gains result in as much as a 20 percent reduction in costs.*[2]

Many organizations have greatly improved their responsiveness through reengineering, six-sigma programs, and other techniques. But there is a limit to the streamlining a company can do through such top-down methods. Most time-saving opportunities are relatively small. Spotting them requires the detailed understanding of how work is done that comes only from actually *doing* it. It is hard for managers to identify all the unnecessary work that employees do, particularly in a white-collar environment. To the employees, however, their wasted time is obvious and irritating.

To understand this, consider the idea submitted by Jennie Rogers, an administrative assistant in the finance department at the MacMillin Corporation, a medium-size construction company in New Hampshire. Every month, frustrated colleagues in the accounting department would come to her for help when trying to reconcile gasoline credit card receipts to customer statements. Fifty different workers and site managers purchased fuel for their vehicles all around New England, using credit cards from seven different companies. Each fuel charge had to be matched with the appropriate construction project. Out of three hundred or so fuel purchases made each month, people would remember to turn in perhaps half the receipts. The accountants needed Rogers's help because her payroll duties gave her access to records of which jobs each driver had been working on. On average, Jennie spent ten to thirteen hours each month tracking down information needed to match up fuel purchases with jobs.

One day, during lunch, she noticed a trade magazine on a table. The cover article was about corporate fueling systems based on a single credit card that was valid at most gasoline stations. To activate the pump, the driver had to enter certain information, including a personal identification number (PIN), a vehicle identification number, and the odometer reading. She realized that this credit card could take care of most of her company's consolidating work automatically. Her boss approved the idea, and once it was implemented, the time she and her accounting colleagues spent reconciling fuel purchases dropped from a total of twenty hours per month to less than two.

It is easy to see why this problem was obvious to Rogers, but not to her bosses. *They* weren't the ones wasting their time every month, and reconciling fuel slips was not part of her job— she was chipping in to help her accounting colleagues.

In general, managers see only a *fraction* of the opportunities to improve cycle time. This may be why the cumulative impact of employee ideas often comes as such a surprise to them. Consider what happened at a large European-based global high-technology company when in 1999 it embarked on an ambitious drive to improve responsiveness. The CEO gave more than one hundred thousand people in one hundred countries eighteen months to cut the time it took them to do *everything* in half. From his perspective, this was an ambitious Jack Welch–like goal. But a year later, the managing director of one of the company's divisions in Scandinavia—a thousand kilometers away from headquarters—confided to us that with all the time-saving ideas that his employees had submitted, his division had been able to meet the goal in only *three months.*

Managing Complexity

In 1985, at the height of Western interest in Japanese management techniques, James Abegglen and George Stalk made an interesting observation in their book *Kaisha: The Japanese Corporation.*[3] They pointed out that U.S. manufacturers were generally more productive than their Japanese counterparts when making products that required relatively few steps. But for products that required large numbers of steps, U.S. companies were far less productive than their Japanese competitors. The authors offered a number of explanations for this phenomenon, but here is one they did not—the one we think most likely.

A large number of steps means increased complexity. More details must be taken care of, more variables are interrelated, more trade-offs have to be made, and more systems and practices have to be meshed smoothly—there are simply more things to go wrong. Managers see only a fraction of all the problems and opportunities that need to be addressed. The more complex the products and processes, the more managers have to rely on their employees to get all the little things right. According to the National Association of Suggestion Systems, in 1985, the average U.S. company got about one idea from every eight employees, of which less than a *third* were actually used. In that same year, the average Japanese worker gave in more than thirty ideas, of which 72 percent were implemented.[4] This disparity gave Japanese companies a huge advantage as far as attention to detail was concerned. We believe the vastly superior ability of Japanese companies in the mid-1980s to get and implement small ideas from their employees explained their generally superior attention to detail, which gave them such a marked advantage in productivity for complex processes.

A superior ability to handle complexity can also enable an organization to do things its competitors simply cannot. Dana's leasing operation, a 1996 winner of the Malcolm Baldrige National Quality Award, provides a good example. Like every other division of the Dana Corporation, it expects at least two ideas from every employee each month. In the late 1990s, one of its clients was being overwhelmed by the complex process of invoicing its customers. This company leased one-hour photo-processing machines to stores across the country. Invoices, broken down by machine, included the lease fee, the number of rolls of film processed, and the amount of chemicals and paper used that month. The process became extremely complicated when billing a nationwide retailer with more than *two thousand* such machines in its stores. The customer did not have the ability to handle all the details involved and soon lost control of the process. It asked Dana to take it over. Now, each month, each one-hour photo machine across the country telephones into the company's computers to report the previous month's processing activities. Dana then generates all the invoices and sends them out. While the customer couldn't handle the complexity of this job, Dana could. In fact, it had little problem with it—it even became a new value-adding service it offered to its *other* customers. As an executive in the leasing operation pointed out to us, "The reason we are capable of doing things like this is the thousands of little employee ideas over time that make the system better, grow it, and change it."

Small ideas also help deal with another type of complexity: all the ramifications, foreseen and unforeseen, of big ideas. As we shall discuss in the next section, big ideas often need many small ideas to make them work. The faster an organization identifies and resolves these smaller issues, the faster it can exploit the full potential of its bigger ideas.

SMALL IDEAS AND RAPID ORGANIZATIONAL LEARNING

In the mid-1990s, the concept of the "learning organization" became popular with managers and business leaders. It held out the promise of making companies significantly more nimble and adaptable. Books such as Peter Senge's *The Fifth Discipline*[5] hit the business best-seller lists, and consulting companies jumped on the new business opportunity. But, in the end, the excitement over the learning organization proved to be surprisingly short-lived.

In our view, the main reason for this falloff in interest was not that it was a flawed concept—it was a very good one—but that its proponents failed to offer much that was practical.

Many managers returned from seminars and presentations on organizational learning fired up by this vision but unable to do anything about it. They had not been given much in the way of practical tools.

The concept that *organizations*, not just people, can learn had been discussed in academe for some time. Almost twenty years earlier, Chris Argyris and Donald Schön, in their 1978 book *Organizational Learning*,[6] had argued that an organization's policies, procedures, systems, and structures, along with its people's "mental maps" of how it works, constitute its "institutional memory." To the extent that problems or opportunities are identified and acted on, and the resulting changes are then captured in this institutional memory, the organization can be said to "learn." This is why getting employee ideas is a key component of managing organizational learning.

Conceptually, Argyris and Schön's treatise can be thought of as deepening the concept of the *learning curve*—a phenomenon that was first documented in the aircraft industry in World War II. Engineers noticed that for every doubling of the total number of a particular airplane that was produced, the manufacturing cost of each dropped by a predictable amount. If the drop was 20 percent, for example, the second airplane would cost 20 percent less than the first; the fourth, 20 percent of the second; the eighth, 20 percent of the fourth; and so on. The more planes a company built, the better it learned how to do so.

Since that time, similar patterns have been observed in fields ranging from mining and construction to software engineering and writing. In many industries, the learning curve is now routinely factored into cost estimates and budgets. Interestingly, it is *not* generally recognized that while a certain amount of learning happens naturally, most does not. Far from being a universal law with the particular learning rate a "given," the rate at which a company learns depends on how well it manages the learning process.

Learning is a cumulative incremental process—it naturally involves small steps of inquiry, information gathering, testing, and feedback. This is why an idea system capable of encouraging and acting on small ideas is really a gigantic learning and development tool. Every idea, even a bad one, incorporates some form of discovery.

Every new product or service represents a form of change, often *big* change. And big change always creates new problems and opportunities that, taken together, define a large part of what the company has to learn. The faster a company can address these, the faster it learns. Take Winnebago Industries, for example. Even though members of the engineering staff spend considerable time on the manufacturing line before, during, and immediately after introducing a new model, they cannot spot every problem. However, many minor design issues and other improvement opportunities are readily apparent to the front-line employees who assemble the vehicles. Following are some employee ideas after one model change, for example:

- A customized steel plate made by a supplier did not fit properly.

- The length of the screws used to attach particular paneling was nearly the thickness of the internal wall, so that when they were tightened down, sometimes indentations were visible in the next room.

- The windows and doors cut out of the walls of the vehicles could be used as substrates for benches or shelves elsewhere in the motor homes.

- Special map pockets, cut out of brand-new dielectric panels, could be cut instead from scrap pieces of this same material from another operation.

But organizational learning covers much more than new product introductions. Any large change creates a myriad of smaller learning opportunities. Consider, for example, what happened at ABB Infosystems, a Scandinavian subsidiary of the Swiss company ABB.

ABB frequently reorganizes to stay close to its customers, and it has become very good at it. During one reorganization of ABB Infosystems, the only person in its Huskvarna, Sweden, main office who had been able to troubleshoot a highly specialized printer for finished customer output was transferred hundreds of kilometers away. No one realized the problem—perhaps not even the employee himself—until the printer acted up several weeks later. Immediately, a suggestion came in to the idea system: Fly the reassigned employee back to the facility to train others. The managing director told us this story to illustrate how much his company had come to depend on its idea system to help handle rapid change. No matter how skilled or careful his managers were, they were bound to miss some details. Without the capability to identify and fix the resulting problems quickly, the fast pace of change at his company would only cause chaos.

Many ideas are learning opportunities. Consider what ABB Infosystems learned by realizing it had transferred away a minor, but nonetheless necessary, skill. Now, it can plan better for such issues in the future. When the company incorporated a more detailed skills assessment into its procedures for restructuring—that is, into its institutional memory—it learned a bit more about how to reorganize smoothly and effectively.

Learning is a cumulative incremental process—it naturally involves small steps of inquiry, information gathering, testing, and feedback. This is why an idea system capable of encouraging and acting on small ideas is really a gigantic learning and development tool. Every idea, even a bad one, incorporates some form of discovery.

SUSTAINABLE COMPETITIVE ADVANTAGE

In the last chapter, we briefly described how small ideas tend to stay proprietary, because there are no mechanisms for competitors to find out about them, and even if they do, the ideas are often situation-specific and so *cannot* be copied. Because of their proprietary nature, they accumulate into a considerable cushion of sustainable competitive advantage. For companies in fiercely competitive industries, this cushion can mean the difference between struggling to survive and being highly successful. The case of Milliken and Company illustrates this point well.

Milliken competes against textile manufacturers operating in some of the poorest countries in the world, which pay their employees less than *one-twentieth* of what Milliken pays its people. The textile industry is mature, and every competitor has access to the same equipment. Consequently, Milliken has to compete by outmanaging its rivals, which it has been doing for several decades, in large part with its OFI ("Opportunity for Improvement") system. The system brought in some seven thousand employee ideas *every working day* in 2002. Because most of these OFIs are small, they are impossible or difficult for competitors to copy.

At one Milliken facility in Denmark, for example, the director showed us a number of machines, each of which had literally hundreds of minor improvements made to it through worker ideas. Cumulatively these had doubled or tripled the machines' speeds and made them capable of doing things their designers had not even thought of. While competitors can easily purchase the same equipment, it will be much harder for them to duplicate the effect of all these improvements. Until its low-wage competitors find ways to promote as many good ideas from their workers, Milliken's OFI system guarantees it significant competitive advantage.

Small ideas are also the key to creating sustainable competitive advantage from big ideas. While big ideas may be readily copied or countered by competitors, the small ideas that exploit them are part of the organization's learning, and remain largely proprietary. The sustainable competitive advantage created by these smaller follow-up ideas may well be *greater* than that of the big idea itself. To understand this more fully, consider what happened at a Dana facility in Cape Girardeau, Missouri.

This facility manufactures axles and gears for light and medium trucks. Its many metal-cutting machines consume tens of thousands of gallons of cutting oil each year. As each cutting tool bites into a part, a continuous spray of oil lubricates and cools it.

For years, a forklift truck had brought cutting oil to each machine in a large plastic tote (a collapsible, thick, fifty-gallon barrel). Each operator would insert a hose into this barrel and pump the oil into his or her machine. With more than a hundred thirsty machines, the company had to dedicate a forklift truck and driver full-time to distributing oil within the facility.

Small ideas tend to stay proprietary, since there are no mechanisms for competitors to find out about them, and even if they do, the ideas are often situation-specific and so cannot be copied. Because of their proprietary nature, they accumulate into a considerable cushion of sustainable competitive advantage. This cushion can mean the difference between struggling to survive and being highly successful.

But in the summer of 1997, an employee suggested that rather than working with totes, why not install a large tank and a system of overhead pipes and *pipe* the oil directly to each machine? The idea had some obvious benefits. First, the operators' work would no longer be disrupted with each forklift delivery, and they could draw oil as needed. Second, the forklift truck could be eliminated and its driver freed up for more value-adding work. The proposal was carefully studied before it was approved. Once the pipes were installed, however, it soon became clear that no one had even begun to anticipate the myriad of opportunities they would create throughout the company.

The first thing that was noticed—obvious in hindsight—was that since the company now bought its oil in *bulk*, the price went down significantly. Moreover, the new tank occupied only half the space that the totes had, so a significant amount of space was freed up. The problem of disposing of empty totes—which because of the residual oil in them were classified as hazardous waste—also disappeared. And when the forklift truck finally stopped making deliveries, another advantage of the new system became apparent. Previously, every few months or so, the forklift would accidentally spear one of the totes and cause a spill. While the cost of the cleanup and the lost oil was minimal, each spill had to be reported to the state environmental authorities, which required considerable paperwork and time.

The idea clearly saved a lot of money. But suppose a competitor had somehow learned—from the oil supplier, for example—that Dana was now buying its oil in bulk. As soon as it installed an oil tank, the competitor would have realized all the direct consequences of the oil tank idea. But it wouldn't necessarily have come up with all the associated small ideas that turned out to be even more valuable.

In the new system, the oil was dispensed through hoses that dropped down from the overhead pipes. Just like fueling a car, the machine operator would squeeze a lever on the nozzle to pump the oil. The nozzles happened to have gauges on their handles. Now, for the first time, the machine operators began to notice *how much* oil their machines were using.

After the cutting oil is sprayed on the tool, the oil runs down into a sump from which it is recirculated. One employee began wondering why, if the oil was being recycled, his machine was consuming so much of it. He realized that the loss was due to the oil-drenched metal shavings that came out of a chute on the side of the machine into a scrap bin. If a two-foot-long sieve was attached to the end of this chute, he proposed, oil would have time to drip through it as the shavings were pushed slowly over it. His idea saved ten gallons per day on his machine. With fourteen other machines in his department, the total savings worked out to 150 gallons per day. The idea quickly got around to people in other departments, who began to submit all kinds of oil-saving ideas for their own equipment, too.

Why did the relatively simple idea for an oil tank have such far-reaching implications? Before it came along, the high cost of cutting oil was an accepted cost of doing business. No one saw it as a problem. But when the nozzles on the oil hoses happened to come with meters, people were alerted to this previously invisible source of waste. In a facility that was averaging thirty-six ideas from each employee every year, this was like throwing a leg of meat to piranhas. And because the waste was eliminated through a series of small ideas, the resulting cost advantage was essentially proprietary.

HOW SMALL IDEAS LEAD TO BIG ONES

In this section, we look at another aspect of the relationship between small and big ideas. Many small ideas are the germs of bigger ideas, although the connections are not always obvious. A big problem or opportunity frequently manifests itself through a host of smaller signs or symptoms, each of which might be seen individually by different people in different places at different times. What might *seem* to be a small idea could in fact be addressing a single facet of this larger issue. To understand this point more fully, let us look at an example.

Monrovia is one of the largest wholesale nurseries in the United States. Its potted plants and trees are sold in stores throughout the country. Shortly after it started its idea system, it got a big idea from a worker at its Azusa, California, location. Yet for several months after it was implemented, neither he nor anyone else realized what its real impact was.

Much of Monrovia's work involves transplanting plants into increasingly larger pots as they grow—a process referred to in the industry as "canning." Some plants may be transplanted four or five times. The soil used is specially formulated for each kind of plant and kept in huge piles outside the canning shed.

Before the worker submitted his idea, the canning job quickly got very unpleasant when it rained. The soil included a healthy dose of "organic fertilizer" (manure), which turned acidic and noxious when wet. It got under peoples' fingernails, irritated their skin, and smelled awful. Moreover, the soil itself became difficult to work with, and after only a few hours, the workers' hands would start to hurt. The employee's idea? Buy tarpaulins to cover the piles of soil whenever it begins to rain. Easy enough. The idea was approved, and the worker was recognized for his "morale-boosting" suggestion.

But nobody anticipated the consequences of his idea for the *plants*. When canning in dry soil, almost 100 percent of plants grow and thrive. No one had realized that with wet soil, the yield drops dramatically, sometimes down to *60 percent*. Because the soil cakes when it dries, it becomes harder for growing roots to penetrate. It also clumps and leaves pockets of air under the surface, exposing the roots, which then cannot properly absorb water and nutrients.

In other words, whenever it rained, the company would unknowingly enter a low-yield phase. Because the plants died gradually and at different rates, Monrovia never realized what was happening. And since the canning lines can transplant up to 2,700 plants per *hour*, and after a heavy rainfall might be working for many hours with wet soil, this idea saved an immense amount of money.

A major problem or opportunity often cuts across organizational lines and manifests itself through multiple symptoms, many of which can be quite subtle. One can never tell who is going to spot which symptom first or how that person will propose to address it. Consequently, the smallest idea might well be a partial reaction to something much bigger. At Monrovia, a manager *might* have noticed a drop in yield during a particularly wet season, or spotted unexpected variances in labor productivity, and somehow connected this with the weather. Or a company horticulturist *might* have noticed a patch of sickly plants, examined them, and seen that their soils were lumpy. But chances are that the response would not have been as quick or decisive as that worker's was.

Understanding how wet soil on the canning lines affects yield was a huge discovery for the company, and it was no accident that it was made by a worker. The immediacy and intensity of the stimulus he got to do something about the offending soil were especially powerful because he was working directly with it. Others in the company might have smelled the manure, but he had it on his clothes, under his fingernails, and in his shoes. And not only did he stink when he went home, his hands hurt. Luckily, although the company's managers were not going home at night in the same state, they understood the value in small ideas from their workforce. And with Monrovia's ability to react to minor symptoms came the ability to address far bigger and deeper issues.

Small ideas are the *best* sources of big ideas. Even the biggest ideas often begin as a sequence of relatively small ones. (Despite the heroic lore of invention, a big idea almost never comes to someone in a single "aha" flash-of-brilliance moment.[7]) The tiniest idea may be the key to something huge. To unlock this potential, managers should get into the habit of asking themselves the following questions.

Question 1. Can this idea be used elsewhere in the organization?   Sometimes a single small improvement idea can be used in many other places, vastly multiplying its initial impact. Unless somebody asks, "Where else can this idea be used?" the opportunity will be missed.

---

*Small ideas are the **best** source of big ideas. A big problem or opportunity frequently manifests itself through a host of smaller signs or symptoms, each of which might be seen individually by different people in different places at different times. What might **seem** to be a small idea could in fact be addressing a facet of this larger issue. This bigger issue can often be discovered by probing with the right questions.*

In the late 1990s, for example, an appliance salesperson in a Chicago branch of one of the largest retailers in the United States figured out a simple way to avoid a problem that often came up after he sold a refrigerator. When it was delivered to the customer's home, it wouldn't always fit through all the necessary doorways. The delivery crew would struggle with it for a while, often damaging it (and the doorways) in the process, before giving up and retreating to the truck, reboxing the refrigerator, and taking it back to the warehouse. Nationwide, the problem was costing the company millions of dollars. In addition to having to pay the delivery crews for failed deliveries, the appliances they damaged had to be marked down. For the salespeople, it meant extra paperwork, angry customers, and perhaps the loss of a sale.

The salesman's solution: Whenever someone bought a refrigerator, he cut a piece of string to the length of its critical dimension and stapled it to the receipt. He told the customer, "When you get home, use this string to check every doorway that your new refrigerator will have to go through. Call me immediately if there is a problem." Other salespeople in his department soon adopted the idea, as did seven or eight of the company's other stores in the region. But consider this: Had the company had a fluid process for communicating good ideas like this between its stores, it could have used this one at more than *two thousand* locations. Because it did not, more than *99 percent* of this idea's potential was squandered.

Question 2. What other ideas does this one suggest?   Every small idea should be eyed as a possible clue to a bigger one. Using the small idea as a stepping stone, a larger problem or opportunity can sometimes be unmasked. Take, for example, Harald's idea at Grapevine Canyon Ranch (table 2.1): "I can translate ride and brochure information into German." Suppose the question had been asked, "What else does this idea make one think of?" Harald stepped forward because German was the language he happened to know. But what about Spanish, French, Japanese, and other languages? Perhaps other employees knew these languages? If not, someone in the community probably did—a local high school teacher, a professional, or perhaps a native speaker who lived locally. And what about Grapevine Canyon's Web site? Couldn't it be set up with different languages, too? Fully explored, Harald's idea could have triggered a general reexamination of the ranch's posture toward international guests. For example, does it offer their favorite foods or drinks? What about providing foreign language classes for employees? Could the ranch provide extra value-adding services for its foreign guests, such as currency exchange, foreign-language DVDs, or cable channels? What about posting critical safety notices in foreign languages, too? Grapevine Canyon already gets a number of foreign visitors, and high growth could come from increasing the resort's attractiveness to them even further.

Harald's small idea was his response to a facet of a much larger opportunity. One can never tell when a small idea might be pointing at a large opportunity in this way. It is good practice to always be alert to the possibility.

Question 3. *Are there any patterns in the ideas that have come in?* Often a significant problem or opportunity gives rise to *multiple* small ideas. The connection between them may be seen in *patterns* in the ideas that have come in.

In 1999, we attended an idea meeting at a national marketing company. Each employee was expected to come to this meeting with an idea to present.

One person pointed out that the company was paying too much for office supplies. Prices were significantly lower at Staples, he told the group. A local supplier had been giving the company a 50 percent discount for years, "But my question is, 50 percent discount from *what?*"

"Thanks for bringing this up," his manager responded. "I'll call purchasing and let them know."

A few minutes later, another employee told of how she had recently attended a computer conference in Denver, traveling with someone from another department. Because they each had different schedules, they had rented separate cars. Interestingly, she had noticed, he had paid twice as much as she did for the same car, from the same rental company. The reason? He used the *corporate* discount, but she had AAA. "I suggest that the company buy a corporate AAA membership. This would not only save a lot of money but would be a nice employee benefit."

"Cool! I'll pass that one along to purchasing, too," the manager responded.

Each of these two ideas taken separately was useful enough. But taken together, they point to a potentially big problem—this company's purchasing department might need a wake-up call. Had only *one* of the ideas come up, this might not have been obvious, and it would have been an overreaction to rush members of the purchasing department off for more negotiation training. But suppose poor purchasing practices did in fact underlie the two price discrepancies the employees identified. It is easy to see how only two ideas, coming within a few minutes of each other, might nudge a thoughtful person into looking for the larger issue underlying them. If the management of this company had been actively looking for patterns in the ideas that came in, it might easily have flagged the problem before it cost the company a lot of money.

It is important for both managers and employees to make a conscious effort to look for connections between the ideas that come in over time. While larger opportunities can be identified by looking for deeper issues in individual ideas, chances are they will be a lot easier to spot from patterns in ideas. Building from multiple related ideas also minimizes the danger of generalizing too much from a single idea.

The Cumulative Impact of a Single "Small" Idea

Small ideas have another important characteristic. Over time, even a seemingly tiny idea—one that saves only a few steps, seconds, cents, or perhaps just a sheet of paper—can have an enormous cumulative impact. When miniscule savings are generated hundreds, thousands, or even millions of times over years, they can add up to a substantial sum. One of our favorite examples of this phenomenon comes from the early days of Standard Oil.

In the early 1870s, when Standard Oil was still relatively small, John D. Rockefeller, the chairman and founder of the company, visited one of its refineries on Long Island. At one point, he inspected a production line where containers were being filled with kerosene for export. Stopping by the machine where the lids were sealed on with solder, he asked a worker how many drops of solder he used.

"Forty," the worker told him. Rockefeller asked him if he could do it with two fewer drops. That didn't work, but it did with *thirty-nine* drops.

Even in retirement, Rockefeller remembered this tiny improvement:

> *That one drop of solder saved $2,500 the first*
> *year; but the export business kept on increasing*
> *after that and doubled, quadrupled—became*
> *immensely greater than it was then; and the saving*
> *has gone steadily along, one drop on each can,*
> *and has amounted since to many hundreds of*
> *thousands of dollars.*[8]

If Rockefeller hadn't had an eye for detail and had overlooked the idea, or thought of it but self-censored it as being too small to bother with, he would have ultimately missed a huge opportunity. As the company grew, the idea continued contributing quietly for decades, drop by drop.

THE TRUE CURRENCY OF MANAGING IDEAS

The final reason to go after small ideas is that they allow an organization to create the right conditions and culture for *all* ideas. Big ideas come along so rarely and unpredictably that they offer little to measure and manage. There are few opportunities for managers to gain experience in managing ideas and for employees to get accustomed to coming up with them and working with them. The prevalent zeal for big ideas explains why many organizations do such a poor job at getting ideas from their people. Without the data and the experience that come from handling lots of ideas, managers have little meaningful feedback on the actions they take. They operate in a haze of half-facts, speculation, and wishful thinking. The decouple from reality that comes with operating without facts can lead managers and organizations to do some embarrassingly flaky things in the name of promoting ideas.

But everyone can be expected to come up with small ideas on a regular basis. The number of ideas provides something to measure and therefore to manage. Simple indicators of performance highlight trouble spots and identify areas where improvements can be made. For example, the number of ideas each manager gets is a good indicator of his or her ability to encourage and act on ideas. In a large Mexican company we worked with, one manager was getting an average of twelve ideas per employee, while his peers were getting only three. The obvious question was, What was he doing that his colleagues were not? Another important thing to know is *who* is giving in ideas and who is not. When an employee is not offering many ideas, it may be that he or she lacks confidence, doesn't get along with his or her manager, or doesn't feel his or her idea will get a fair hearing. Or perhaps he or she is angry or resentful about something. Whatever the problem, it is rare that the employee doesn't have any ideas about how to make his or her own job easier or how to improve the company in some way.

---

*Big ideas come along so rarely and unpredictably that they offer little to measure and manage. There are few opportunities for managers to gain experience in managing ideas and for employees to learn how to come up with them. But **everyone** can be expected to come up with small ideas on a regular basis. This provides something to measure and therefore to manage.*

Sometimes entire *categories* of employees submit relatively few ideas, indicating a deeper, more systemic problem. For example, in the late 1990s, data from the Swedish Institute for Suggestion Systems showed that women in that country, perhaps the most egalitarian in the world, were giving in ideas at only 10 percent of the rate of men. Sweden is heavily unionized, and the unions have national labor contracts that govern how employee ideas should be handled. Obviously, something in these rules was discriminatory. How could Swedish companies have become aware of the problem without tracking who came up with ideas? Once they were aware of it, they could address it, and the data would then tell them about the progress of their efforts.

A constant flow of small ideas gets everyone accustomed to dealing with them as a regular part of their work. People grow accustomed to experiencing change and to seeing the benefits of it. Consequently, when someone *does* have a big idea, he or she is far more likely to step forward with it, and his or her manager is far more likely to welcome it and handle it well. And when employees see managers responding to changes they initiate, the whole organization becomes much less resistant to *management-initiated* change as well. In short, the ability to listen to small ideas creates a more flexible, responsive, and adaptive company, while improving trust, respect, communication, and involvement.

Once an organization creates an environment in which small ideas are valued, few people want to go back to what they had previously. Employees can address problems and opportunities they could not have before, and their work lives become less frustrating and more interesting. Managers discover that employee ideas can help them to get the results they need. And instead of being preoccupied with firefighting, managers have time to focus on their real jobs—longer-term improvement and planning for the future. As Julian Richer puts it:

> *Before I introduced the suggestions scheme at Richer Sounds, I probably used to come up with 90% of the ideas for improving the company and that was hard work. It felt like pushing a wagon uphill.*
>
> *Now 90% of the suggestions come from staff and I am sitting on the wagon, being pulled up the hill.*[9]

KEY POINTS

- Managers are often primarily interested in "home run" ideas—those worth millions of dollars or leading to breakthrough innovations. But in many respects, small ideas are more valuable than big ones.

- Large numbers of small ideas allow an organization to reach levels of performance that are otherwise unachievable. Without them, it is impossible to attain excellence.

- Small ideas are the primary tool for organizational learning. The ability to tap them moves an organization onto a faster learning curve.

- Small ideas provide far more sustainable competitive advantage than big ones, because unlike big ideas, they tend to remain proprietary.

- Often the only lasting competitive advantage from a big idea comes from all the small ideas that exploit the further opportunities it creates.

- Small ideas are the best source of big ideas, if one knows how to ask the right questions about them.

- Big ideas come along so rarely and unpredictably that they offer little to measure and manage. But because employees can be expected to come up with small ideas on a regular and consistent basis, these provide organizations with something measurable that allows them to truly *manage* their employees' ideas, and so create profound change.

GUERRILLA TACTICS

Five actions you can take today (without the boss's permission)

1. Just ask. Ask your people to come to their regular department meetings with one small idea that will make their work easier or improve the company in some way and that will not require permission from above or significant resources to implement. Have each person present his or her idea, and ask the group to discuss it and build on it. If an idea is worthwhile, agree on who will implement it.

2. Offer lunch. Bring in pizza (or whatever food is appropriate), and collect and discuss your employees' ideas over an extended lunch. Hold the lunch off-site, if more appropriate. Such a lunch can become a regular activity.

3. When change occurs, ask for ideas. Whenever major change occurs or is anticipated, encourage your group to be on the lookout for the new problems and opportunities created by this change, and to offer ideas to address them.

4. Look for that bigger problem or opportunity in a small idea. When an idea comes in that might have broader implications, explore them. Together with your people, identify the larger issues involved, and decide what can be done to address them.

5. Work on reluctant participants. When a person is not offering any ideas, talk to him or her and find out why. Encourage and help this person until he or she feels comfortable and confident about giving in ideas.

CHAPTER 3

THE PITFALLS OF REWARDS

*But doesn't the widespread use of rewards suggest . . .
that they work? Why would a failed strategy be preferred? . . .
The negative effects appear over a longer period of time,
and by then their connection to the reward may not be at
all obvious. The result is that rewards keep getting used.*

—Alfie Kohn, Punished by Rewards[1]

Whenever managers begin seeking ideas from their employees, the issue of rewards inevitably pops up. The natural, and seemingly the fairest, thing to do is to reward each idea according to its value. This makes eminent sense to everyone and is, in fact, what many organizations end up doing. The most common schemes offer a percentage—usually between 5 and 25 percent—of the first year's savings or profit from each idea. With such an incentive in place, all managers have to do is sit back and wait for the ideas to pour in. The problem is, they don't.

Perhaps the most counterintuitive and certainly the least well-known aspect of managing ideas is how counterproductive seemingly "commonsense" reward schemes can be. In his widely cited article "On the Folly of Rewarding A, While Hoping for B,"[2] Steven Kerr writes:

> *Whether dealing with monkeys, rats, or human beings, it is hardly controversial to state that most organisms seek information concerning what activities are rewarded, and then seek to do (or at least pretend to do) those things, often to the virtual exclusion of activities not rewarded. . . . Numerous examples exist of reward systems that are fouled up in that the types of behavior rewarded are those which the rewarder is trying to discourage, while the behavior desired is not being rewarded at all.*

In our experience, few managers are aware of the pitfalls in rewards and how they can easily undermine the very behaviors they are supposed to promote. This lack of awareness explains why so many organizations set up dysfunctional reward schemes, without ever realizing anything is wrong. After all, however bad the reward scheme is, it will generate *some* ideas. And when it does, it is only natural to credit the ideas to the rewards being offered. Unfortunately, the far greater number of ideas that are *discouraged* by the very same reward scheme go unseen and unmeasured. Few notice their absence, and even fewer connect that absence to the real problem.

■————————————

SOME INCONVENIENT EVIDENCE

At first, we, like so many others, assumed that the best way to encourage ideas was to reward each one according to its worth. The
bigger the idea, the bigger the reward. It seemed self-evident
that the more generous the percentage payouts, the more ideas
would flow in. But in the late 1980s, we came across some surprising data that caused us to reexamine this simplistic viewpoint
(see table 3.1). Japanese companies were getting extraordinary
numbers of ideas from their employees, far more than their U.S.
competitors, but without the heavy emphasis on rewards.[3]

How was it that American companies were paying rewards
more than *two hundred times* greater than their Japanese counterparts, but getting less than a *three-hundredth* of the number
of ideas? How was it that almost *nine* out of *ten* Japanese ideas
were used while less than a *third* of American ideas were? How
could it be that Japanese employees were so much more interested than their American counterparts in making suggestions,
as shown by the participation rates? The bottom line was clear:

Table 3.1. Comparative idea data from the United States and Japan in 1989

	Japan	United States
Number of ideas per employee	37.4	0.12
Participation rate	77.6%	9%
Adoption rate	87.3%	32%
Average net savings per adoption	$126	$6,114
Net savings per 100 employees	$422,100	$22,825
Average reward per adopted idea	$2.83	$602

Japanese companies were realizing overall net savings per employee some *twenty times* more than the American companies.

All this seemed odd to us. It was the opposite of what we would have expected. Our first reaction was no different from that of most Westerners who saw these strange numbers. We, too, were sure that *cultural* differences were the cause of the disparity. But that convenient explanation did not hold up for long once we began looking more deeply into the matter.

In the late 1980s and early 1990s, Alan Robinson studied the idea systems of twenty large Japanese companies firsthand. From the beginning, it was obvious that these companies were managing ideas very differently from their U.S. counterparts. And the more we learned about the history of how Japanese companies developed their processes to manage ideas, the harder it became to attribute the many differences with Western practices to "culture." Just as had happened in the quality field, *American* experts had played a pivotal role in the inception of high-performing idea systems in Japan shortly after World War II. What seemed so alien to Americans in the 1980s that it had to have come from a foreign culture had in fact originated with leading management thinkers in their own country.

By the early 1990s, North American transplants of Japanese companies using identical minimal-reward philosophies were getting large numbers of ideas from their employees—*more*, in some cases, than their parent companies back home. By the mid-1990s, a handful of American and European companies with no organizational ties to Japan were doing just as well, too, with the same approach to rewards. By the late 1990s, some of the best idea systems in the world were outside Japan. Worldwide, the pattern was the same—monetary rewards for individual ideas were deemphasized or even *eliminated*. Why was this?

Because the managers involved understood the real reasons why employees step forward with ideas.

─────■─────────────

WHY DO PEOPLE STEP FORWARD WITH IDEAS?

Why would people offer ideas without the prospect of rewards? What's in it for them? The answers to these questions go to the heart of why so many companies have found rewards both unnecessary and counterproductive.

Most people already *have* lots of ideas for their organizations, *want* to tell managers about them, and would be *thrilled* to see them used. An idea starts when a person becomes aware of a problem or opportunity. The definition of a problem is "a source of perplexity, distress, or vexation." It is something people have a natural inclination to fix. An opportunity—defined as "a time, place, or condition favoring advancement or progress"— quickly becomes a source of frustration to someone who spots it, if the organization is missing it. It *bothers* that person. In other words, employees will naturally come up with a great number of ideas—whether it is to make their jobs easier or less frustrating, to stop their organizations wasting money, or simply because they see an opportunity to do something better. Consider the following example.

In 2000, Art Samson worked in the Denver center of the Defense Finance and Accounting Service (DFAS). His group handled the payroll for some five hundred thousand U.S. Air Force personnel. One of its responsibilities was to send out roughly 460,000 "allotment" checks each month—payments that Air Force personnel could arrange to be deducted from their wages and forwarded to predesignated parties. These payments could be for anything: bills, alimony, or extra money for a spouse or aging parent.

About fifty times a month, people would call Samson's department about a missing check. Before issuing a new one, it was necessary to verify that the original had not already been cashed. Roughly 75 percent of the time, it had been.

Each caller was asked to send a signed letter detailing the claim. DFAS attached this letter to a form and mailed it to the U.S. Treasury in Washington, D.C. (By law, the Treasury Department writes almost all checks for the federal government.) Some forty-five days later, the response would arrive. If the check hadn't been cashed, payment on it would be stopped and a new check ordered. If it had been cashed, Treasury would send a photocopy of its front and back. By comparing the signature on the check with that on the claimant's letter, DFAS could tell whether that person had cashed it. If someone else had cashed it, the case was forwarded for investigation to the Treasury and the check reissued.

Each case took about half an hour to deal with. Fifty cases a month meant about twenty-five hours of staff time. Furthermore, people who had lost or not received their checks had to wait two months for another one. And every month, three or four people, fed up with waiting for a response, would call their representatives in Congress. When a congressional inquiry came in, DFAS had seventy-two hours to respond. In that time, Samson's group had to document the case thoroughly, write a report on it, and the director of the center had to review and sign it.

One day after work, Samson went out for a beer with a friend who had once worked at the Treasury Department and happened to ask him about the search requests. Samson learned that the front and back of every cashed check were scanned into a computer system. When a search request came in, a clerk printed out the image of the check and mailed it back. Samson had an idea: Why couldn't his group get direct access to this system?

Most people already have lots of ideas for their organizations, want to tell managers about them, and would be thrilled to see them used. An idea starts when a person becomes aware of a problem or opportunity. The definition of a problem is "a source of perplexity, distress, or vexation." It is something people have a natural inclination to fix.

He went to his director, who liked the idea, and together they approached Treasury. As might be expected, their request met with resistance, particularly since the Privacy Act obliged the Treasury Department to keep information out of unauthorized hands. Outsiders had *never* been given access to its system. Being designed only for internal use, there were no firewalls around the DFAS data. Once logged in, a DFAS employee would be able to access information about many *other* types of federal checks, too. It took eighteen months of bureaucratic wrangling to persuade Treasury to modify its system so that DFAS could access it securely. Today, most lost-check claims are processed while the caller is still on the telephone. Furthermore, since DFAS/Denver began using the Treasury system, there has not been a single congressional inquiry.

Samson didn't think of his idea or champion it for a year and a half to get a reward. He simply wished to eliminate an annoying problem. The truth is that most people step forward with ideas because they want to. They feel pride in their work, enjoy making a difference, and appreciate it when others recognize what they have done.

It is one thing to realize that employees don't have to be bribed to give in ideas. But one might think that the prospect of getting a share of the benefits from their ideas would only *increase* their natural motivation. In practice, however, most such schemes backfire. The more money a company dangles in front of its employees, the fewer ideas it gets, and the more problems it creates for itself.

■

THE INVISIBLE COSTS OF REWARDS

Be careful with money. It can ruin relationships. We appreciated the wisdom in this advice all the more as we developed an understanding of all the problems that organizations create for themselves when they try to reward individual ideas according to each one's worth. It is amazing how one can get into so much trouble by doing what seems so simple and logical.

The Measurement Problem

In 1997, Jean-François Lefresne, an Air France mechanic at Orly Airport in Paris, came up with a big money-saving suggestion. It won a Trophée d'Innovation for one of the best ideas in the airline that year. The story is this: When airplanes come in for major overhauls, maintenance crews must routinely remove screws that are locked in place with corrosion, particularly in areas that tend to get wet, such as the bottom thresholds of doors. Before Lefresne's idea, the high torque of the power tools used would often twist the heads off these unyielding screws. When this happened, it took several hours to drill out the body of the screw, retap the hole, put a new screw in, and get the work approved and signed off.

Lefresne's idea almost completely eliminated this problem. It was based on a standard garden tool used for digging fence post holes. That tool, a kind of giant apple corer on the end of a long shaft, is designed so that a person can stand on it and twist it around to drive it down into the earth. Lefresne realized that if he mounted a screwdriver on the bottom of a similar tool, he could then stand on the recalcitrant screw, break the seal of corrosion with *downward* force, and apply the necessary torque more gradually and with more control. When Air France adopted his idea, the number of broken screws dropped dramatically.

Had Air France offered rewards for ideas, it would have been a nightmare trying to calculate how much Lefresne's suggestion was worth. Its mechanics have to remove *hundreds* of corroded screws each year. (Air France Industries does the heavy maintenance for many airlines around the world.) To figure out how much time and money was saved by just this *one* idea, someone would have had to determine the total number of broken screws per year systemwide, estimate the cost of each occurrence (including any aircraft downtime), and—most difficult of all—make a stab at how many fewer would now be broken. It is unlikely that maintenance records are kept in a way that would make this task easy. Furthermore, all this work would be non–value adding— its sole purpose would be to determine Lefresne's reward.

Worse, since the calculated savings would be both an *approximation* and a *projection*, they would be open to dispute. Had Air France offered rewards based on the value of ideas, Lefresne might well have spent his time drafting memos about how much his idea actually saved, rather than moving on to his next one. A number of managers at companies that offer percentage rewards have told us that they systematically *inflate* the value of ideas, so as to avoid disputes. Still, they can't avoid them entirely. When money is at stake, these disputes can get quite contentious and cause considerable ill feeling and distrust. A company that gives significant rewards for individual ideas needs some extra procedures in place that Air France does not—namely, an *evaluation* process to estimate projected savings from each idea, an *arbitration* process to settle disputes over these calculations, and an *audit* process to make sure that the reported savings are accurate.

It is one thing to realize that employees don't have to be bribed to give in ideas. But one might think that the prospect of getting a share of the benefits from their ideas would only increase their natural motivation. In practice, however, most such schemes backfire. The more money a company dangles in front of its employees, the fewer ideas it gets, and the more problems it creates for itself.

But even with such processes in place, another problem arises. Because only the ideas with readily documentable savings or revenue earn rewards, employees soon become condi-

Figure 3.1 The quantifiability of ideas

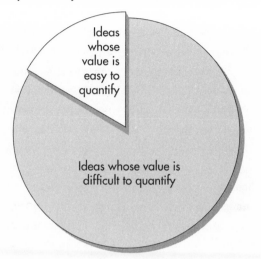

tioned to look exclusively for ideas like these. At the same time that they are being exhorted to "think outside the box," they are being boxed in by rewards that focus them on a very narrow set of problems and opportunities. The reward scheme, that is, unwittingly puts blinders on employees.

Ideas with readily quantifiable cost savings represent only a *small part* of what is possible—even in financial terms. Many ideas with substantial bottom-line impact cannot be quantified. An organization that limits itself to only ideas with readily quantifiable value misses out on *most* of the potential performance improvement from employee ideas, as figure 3.1 illustrates. To understand this better, consider, for example, what turned out to be a very big idea at Grapevine Canyon Ranch.

While searching the Internet, a secretary noticed that most search engines put Grapevine's Web site well down their lists.

Because she maintained her own Web site at home, she happened to know that, all other things being equal, search engines tend to return the most recently updated site. She proposed that the company post a "Horse of the Day" on its Web site, to keep it current. Now, every morning, the office manager leans out of her window, picks a horse in the paddock, takes a picture of it with a digital camera, and uploads it to the Web site. This simple change had an enormous effect on Grapevine's Internet visibility. (Piggybacking on this, another idea was to post daily weather reports, to entice potential customers from northern climates to Arizona's warm temperature and abundant sunshine.)

Even though this idea had a huge impact on the resort, with reservations going up markedly, how could the company begin to put a price on it? How could it tease apart the effect of this single change to its Web site from the rest of its marketing initiatives and from the myriad of other factors that influence its reservation rates?

And even if an idea has no financial impact whatsoever, it might still be very worthwhile. At BIC Corporation, for example, an employee noticed that the heavy burlap bags, in which parts arrived for production, were just being thrown away. The employee suggested that the Red Cross could use them as sand bags for floods. When contacted, the Red Cross said it would be happy to accept all the bags that BIC could provide.

The Problem of Fairness

Every improvement or innovation begins with an idea. But an idea is only a *possibility*—a small beginning that must be nurtured, developed, engineered, tinkered with, championed, tested, implemented, and checked. And even then, it may prove to be only the start of a further evolutionary process that extends, refines, and combines it with other ideas, in order to exploit its potential in different and unexpected ways. Many people could be involved in making the idea happen. In practice, however, it is too difficult and divisive to offer rewards to people other than those who *conceive* the idea. That is, the rewards are for taking the first step in the creative process, which is often the easiest part. All the hard work and creativity that come afterward are ignored. This can be very unfair.

In March 1971, James Lisec and Krishan Jagga, two employees of United Airlines, submitted a suggestion that increased the company's profits by at least $3 million per year. At the time, they had no idea that the fight over the reward for it would change their lives profoundly, turn into a series of bitter and contentious court cases that would drag on for more than twenty years, and end up several times at the California Supreme Court.

Oddly enough, United agreed that Lisec and Jagga had played the key enabling role in the idea.[4] However, its position was that they were not entitled to the $300,000 reward they expected—10 percent of the value of the idea—because the airline had received many similar suggestions before theirs, even though it had rejected them. But when the two men presented their version of the idea, they made a different and stronger case for it, and they were very persistent in persuading key managers of its merits. They made it *happen*.

In 1971, Lisec was a personnel manager and Jagga an industrial engineer at the San Francisco maintenance base. Their idea was to offer discounted fares to employees of the major airlines and their families—50 percent off reserved seats, 80 percent off standby seats—in order to fill seats that would otherwise fly empty. Other major airlines, such as TWA and PanAm, did this, and United already discounted fares for its *own* people as an employee benefit.

Through the years, United had received many suggestions to extend this benefit to employees of other carriers. But all of them had been rejected by the middle managers asked to evaluate them. Lisec and Jagga's mission was to get their company to look at reduced rate travel in terms of *profits*, rather than as an employee benefit. Considerable additional revenue could be generated from employees of *other* airlines buying tickets on United.

For six months, Lisec and Jagga battled various middle managers who blocked their idea. But everything changed on October 10, 1971, when John Stilwell, a union committee member, approached Edward Carlson, then president of United, at a reception after a speech Carlson had given to the International Association of Machinists. Stilwell knew about the difficulty Lisec and Jagga were having with their idea and told Carlson about it. Carlson thanked Stilwell and forwarded a copy of Lisec and Jagga's proposal to a senior vice president in the rate department, over the heads of the managers who had been blocking ideas about discounted rates for years. In November 1971, this department confirmed the correctness of Lisec and Jagga's analysis.

On January 3, 1972, eleven weeks after Stilwell had button-holed Carlson, the corporate policy committee approved a plan for discounted rates for airline employees that differed only in minor details from Lisec and Jagga's proposal. Imagine their disappointment when they learned that instead of getting a 10 percent reward, they were to be given a $1,000 "Impetus Award," to be split between them. The money was to recognize their efforts in *championing* the idea.

Lisec and Jagga filed a grievance. When it was turned down in 1973, they filed a lawsuit. In the summer of 1975, a jury awarded them $1.8 million in damages, later reduced to $400,000 by the judge. United appealed, and in 1979, the appeals court reversed the decision, ruling that the rewards were clearly intended for those who *suggested* the idea first, not for those who championed it.

---

*Most reward schemes pay only for **having** the idea. This is the most identifiable, discrete, and easily measured part of the idea process, though it often requires less creativity and effort than some of the other steps. If rewards are to be given, doesn't **everyone** who plays a role in fulfilling an idea deserve one? Why should some get a reward and others not?*

The two men petitioned for a rehearing, which was denied, and then for a hearing before the California Supreme Court. Shortly after this, too, was denied, they were fired. The reasons, they were told, were the negative publicity generated by a *Wall Street Journal* article on the case and the opening and closing statements of their attorney Marvin Lewis. (Since he was their lawyer, the airline argued, Lisec and Jagga bore responsibility for his remarks.) The two men sued for wrongful discharge.

When this case came to trial six years later in 1985, a jury awarded them a total of $2,979,000 in damages—$479,000 for breach of contract (i.e., back wages) plus $2.5 million in punitive damages for "retaliatory firing in violation of public policy, breach of the implied covenant of good faith and fair dealing, and intentional infliction of emotional distress."[5] United appealed, and in August 1990, the appeals court disallowed the punitive damages but let the breach-of-contract damages stand. The back and forth continued until November 1992, when United's last appeal to the California Supreme Court was denied. Finally, after almost twenty years of expensive and exhausting litigation, it was over. And no one had really won.

The real problem all along, of course, had been the reward scheme. At the same time that it forced United to do what it did, it managed to make Lisec and Jagga feel that the company was going out of its way to split hairs over definitions in order to avoid paying them what they deserved. It is not hard to see why.

Ideas have no value until they are implemented. What companies should really be trying to encourage, therefore, are *completed* ideas. Generally, an idea goes through a number of stages and involves a number of different people:

1. Someone comes up with the idea.

2. It may require some work to develop a good case for it.

3. The idea is championed to management and to those who will be affected by it.

4. It may need further development, refining, and pilot-testing.

5. It may also need formal approval from appropriate authorities.

6. It has to be implemented.

7. The actual effect of the idea must be assessed.

8. Customers, suppliers and employees have to be helped to "buy in" to the change.

Almost all reward schemes are like United's: They pay only for stage 1—that is, *having* the idea. This is the most identifiable, discrete, and easily measured part of the process, though it often requires less creativity and effort than some of the other steps. It had been relatively easy to see the advantages of discounted fares at United—the airline had received more than fifteen suggestions on the topic in the previous three years, and other major airlines already offered them. But it had been relatively *hard* to develop the right case for discounted fares and champion it. Only Lisec and Jagga had succeeded in doing this. To them, it seemed downright unfair to be denied the reward.

Doesn't *everyone* who plays a role in fulfilling an idea deserve a reward? Why should some get a reward and others not? Unfortunately, some contributions are hard to distinguish and evaluate. How much was Lisec and Jagga's championing worth? How hard did the people who implemented the idea have to work, above and beyond what their normal jobs required? In short, it would be a nightmare to apportion credit. And whatever numbers the company might have come up with, they might well have seemed unfair to someone and led to further disputes. This is why most organizations that reward ideas individually stick to rewarding only the people who think up the ideas.

But then they alienate others needed to pull off ideas. The most obvious symptoms of this are bottlenecks in evaluating and implementing ideas. The people needed for these tasks, which can be very time-consuming, often resent them. Why should they figure out how to make *someone else's* raw idea workable, when that person will get both the credit and the reward for it? This resentment creates distrust and contributes to an organization-wide reluctance to deal with suggestions.

We encountered a particularly poignant example of this at a large U.S. vehicle manufacturer, where the engineering department routinely ignored front-line ideas—no matter how good they were. One worker (a grandmother, as she proudly told us) was given parts that *wouldn't fit* on the vehicles coming down the assembly line, because the engineering department had specified the wrong locations for holes in these parts. She had set up a table at her workstation and had brought in her own drill to *redrill* the holes herself, all the time hurrying to keep up with the line.

---

*Ideas come up and are implemented through many different channels. If rewards are offered for any stage of the process in any single channel, to be fair, shouldn't they be offered for **every** stage in **all** of the channels? How can employees be expected to participate wholeheartedly in team-based initiatives, if they can make more money for keeping their ideas to themselves and turning them into the idea system later?*

Twice she submitted a suggestion to fix the part, and twice it was rejected by engineering. Only on the third attempt, after talking with a senior operations manager, was she able to get an engineer to come down and look at it. Even then, rather than correcting the problem immediately, the engineering department refused to change the print until the contract was renewed with the supplier. While workers thought the engineers were arrogant and stupid for resisting even the most obvious improvement suggestions, it bothered the engineers that workers were being paid substantial *bounties* to second-guess their designs. A number of engineers were also convinced that workers weren't disclosing many design-related problems during the new model shakedown period, because improvement ideas submitted during this period were not eligible for rewards.

A number of companies have attempted to extend rewards to employees for evaluating and implementing other people's ideas, only to find themselves faced with a fresh set of problems. Even *greater* resources and overhead are needed to measure and track all the relevant contributions, and to dole out the rewards. Moreover, the rewards send conflicting and dysfunctional signals. Why should someone be paid extra to help with one idea, because it happens to come from a worker eligible for a reward, but not for another idea because it came from a manager or a process improvement team?

Ideas come up and are implemented through many different channels. If rewards are offered for any stage of the process in any single channel, to be fair, shouldn't they be offered for *every* stage in *all* of the channels? How can employees be expected to participate wholeheartedly in team-based initiatives, if they can make more money for keeping their ideas to themselves and turning them in to the idea system later?

When managers reward only quantifiable ideas, fairness becomes an issue in another way: It puts some employees in better positions than others to make considerable extra money. In any organization, there are places of great potential to originate ideas with high quantifiable value, places of almost no potential, and everything in between. The closer the job is to the company's "value streams"—that is, where the money is earned and spent—the easier it is to come up with rewardable ideas. At one major U.S. airline, for example, 60 percent of ideas came from mechanics, some of whom made more money from their ideas than their regular work. Aircraft parts are very expensive, and a relatively minor observation—"Strengthen this part a little and it will last far longer" or "Switch suppliers for that part"—can translate into huge savings and tens of thousands of dollars in rewards.

How Rewards Tempt Managers to Behave Badly

One of the serious problems with the Soviet Union's "rationalization proposal" system—the idea system mandated by Stalin for almost every organization in the country—was that when a worker came up with a big idea, it put his or her managers in danger. If the suggestion saved ten tons of steel per year, for example, instead of being praised for good leadership, the factory manager was more likely to be asked by higher-ups why he hadn't pointed it out before. Was he simply incompetent, or was he committing *economic sabotage,* deliberately undermining his country's effort to catch up with the West? Economic sabotage was one of the most serious crimes in the Soviet Union and was a charge frequently used by the Communist Party in its purges, because it was so difficult to refute.

This problem would not have existed without the presence of rewards. Without rewards, the source of an idea would not have mattered. A significant idea from a worker would simply have been implemented. Its benefit would have shown up in the aggregate performance of the factory and made its director look good.

Few managers in the rest of the world worry about being *executed* when a subordinate comes up with a significant idea. But they do worry about what it makes superiors think of them, and this concern can cause them to behave unethically. We came across a particularly shameful example of this in a large European wireless communications company. In 1997, an employee discovered an error in the billing process that was causing the company to lose track of a significant percentage of international calls and fail to bill customers for them. He submitted a simple idea to fix the problem. The missing annual revenue was estimated to be at least $26 million, although no one really knows the exact amount; in fact, management didn't really *want* to know it.

Another perverse consequence of rewarding individual ideas is that the potentially large sums of money involved can lead to unethical behavior and even outright fraud. People steal each other's ideas, and game and manipulate the system for personal advantage.

Under the rules of the company's idea system, once the idea was implemented, the suggester would be owed 50 percent of the first year's revenue from it—in this case some $13 million. At the time we visited the company, top management had been "evaluating" the idea for several years. The idea system manager was furious. The CEO would rather continue losing $26 million per year, he told us, than risk the embarrassment that might ensue from having to pay such a large reward. The sheer size of the oversight would make any manager reluctant to admit that it had happened on his or her watch. A $13 million reward would have been the largest in European history and would have come to the attention of his board. Also, it might well have been picked up by the media. Think of the negative publicity: Not only had management failed to bill customers to the tune of

$26 million per year, but it had to pay millions more to discover its blunder. It is easy to see why the CEO wanted the idea buried.

There are other reasons why managers sometimes balk at paying out large rewards, even though they made the rules in the first place. However great the organization-wide savings will be from the idea, the reward has to come out of someone's budget, and for that person, it is a large expense. And since managers are always under pressure to keep expenses down, the temptation is to skimp on a significant reward or even back out of it entirely. We have been astonished at the imagination some managers have shown in doing this. Consider, for example, the unusually brazen management team at one of Europe's largest automotive suppliers.

In the late 1990s, the company was having difficulty with an important customer, a prominent European automaker. The problem was that a cooling system it made for engine oil wasn't able to keep the engine from overheating. The customer had made it clear that unless the problem was solved quickly, it would take its business elsewhere. Luckily, a worker sent in a clever idea. He had realized that the oil wasn't circulating through the radiator properly. He suggested putting some curved tubes and baffles inside it to make the oil spiral and swirl as it moved through. His idea improved the heat transfer capacity enough to make the cooling system work, and because of it the company retained tens of millions of euros of business.

The employee eagerly anticipated his reward of 50 percent of the first year's value of his idea—potentially hundreds of thousands of euros. In an astonishing display of ingratitude, the company argued that he wasn't entitled to any money, because his fix had only made the radiator more expensive. Furthermore, he was told, if *he* hadn't thought of this idea, the company would have come up with a fix sooner or later. It was treated as an idea with "noneconomic" benefit, and the worker was given enough "points" for a trip to an auto exhibition in Geneva.

Whatever other harm rewards do, one should never lose sight of their corrupting effect on the *giver* and how they undermine the trust and respect necessary to run an organization well.

How Rewards Can Lead to Fraud

As the saying goes, "If money can be made by doing something wrong, someone will." Another perverse consequence of rewarding individual ideas is that the prospect of large sums of money can lead to outright fraud. Although it is impossible to estimate the full extent of the problem, since most companies don't want these kinds of crimes made public, based on our experience, it is far from uncommon.

A midsize electronics company had a special committee whose job was to select the best suggestion each quarter. The person with the winning idea was given 10 percent of the money it saved. The committee was composed of managers from sales, finance, human resources, engineering, and manufacturing. The most influential person in this group was the director of manufacturing, because of his position, expertise, and more than twenty years with the company. Unfortunately, he was also shaking down the winners for a payoff. His scam was to approach the person whom he considered to have the most lucrative idea and offer to "put in the fix" for it, in return for half of the resulting reward.

One quarter he happened to approach a new employee who asked for a little time to think the proposition over. Because he couldn't believe that the company would condone the manager's behavior, he went to the head of human resources, who quietly alerted the head of accounting.

A fraud investigator was brought in under the cover of being a consultant, charged with taking an "overall look" at the organization. For several months, she conducted interviews with employees and managers, invariably steering the conversation at some point to the suggestion system and asking how they felt it worked. Slowly, the story emerged. When she confronted the director of manufacturing with the evidence, he confessed. Over the years, it turned out, he had stolen some $225,000 from the winning suggesters. As the investigator remarked to us:

I think the majority of front-line workers were aware of what was going on. My impression was that middle and upper management were the only ones who were not. The front-line workers thought either that it was being condoned by executive management or that executive management was so stupid that it was completely in the dark. Either way, they had no faith or trust in it. And that led to low morale throughout the entire company.

This manager got away with his fraud for more than three years, but it was almost inevitable that he would be caught. Too many people knew about it. Most reward-related fraud is harder to detect, because it is more subtle and creative. Consider the following example.

A supervisor in the shipping department of a large garment manufacturer came up with a particularly ingenious scheme. At one point he submitted what appeared to be series of brilliant ideas that dramatically boosted the productivity of his department—but only because he had carefully *sabotaged* its efficiency over the previous six months. He did this by rejecting a large proportion of the garments that arrived in the warehouse and sending them over to quality assurance. Because the quality department was notoriously slow, this effectively took the clothes out of the production cycle for months. After establishing a lower level of shipping productivity, he made a few modest changes to the shipping process and stopped rejecting garments. Management was delighted with the surge in goods moving through the shipping department and rewarded him with 5 percent of the value of his "ideas," or some $6,000.

His scheme unraveled because a random inventory audit found hundreds of boxes of garments in the quality assurance department that didn't match up with inventory records. Not only did the department have far more inventory than it should have had, but none of the stated contents of the boxes matched what was inside.

Unfortunately for the shipping department supervisor, he hadn't anticipated how the quality manager would react to the flood of rejected garments. To him, this meant there was a big quality problem somewhere. Since he had no idea where it was, he tried to hide its presence by concealing the mountain of rejected clothing until he could discover what was wrong.

Once the quality manager had confessed, it didn't take long to discover that there was actually nothing wrong with the garments in question and that the same name was on all the rejection slips. When confronted with this, the supervisor admitted what he had done and was immediately fired.

In both of these cases, it was not regular employees who defrauded the idea system but *managers*. This is not to say that front-line employees are not corrupted by rewards—we often come across cases of them stealing each other's ideas, grossly overstating the value of their ideas, or gaming and manipulating the system. But managers are in much better positions to commit reward-related fraud.

REWARD SYSTEMS THAT WORK

After all the dysfunction we have described with percentage rewards for individual ideas, managers might be tempted to shy away from offering *any* rewards whatsoever. But it is perfectly possible to avoid these problems and still explicitly share with employees the benefits from their ideas. In this section, we describe how a number of companies that have been very successful at getting ideas from their employees also pay out substantial sums of money to them, far more than they would typically earn under a traditional reward scheme. The rewards these organizations give work with, rather than against, the reasons employees *already want* to give in ideas.

Before we discuss their approaches, however, it is important to point out that rewards are truly *optional.* Employees will step forward with plenty of ideas without them. The most powerful incentive to hand in an idea is the knowledge that it will be given a fair hearing and will be implemented if it is recognized as a good one. The best reward system a company can set up is a process that assures ideas are handled quickly, effectively, and smoothly. This is why Idemitsu Kosan (whose idea system has consistently been ranked as one of the best in Japan) and Milliken (which gets more ideas per employee than any other U.S. or European company we are aware of) offer *no* extra rewards for ideas. The financial benefits are shared implicitly, through greater job security and better wages.

But if managers do want to explicitly share some of the financial benefits of employees' ideas with them, they can do so without creating the rap sheet of problems we discussed earlier in this chapter. In fact, a good reward system can create useful *synergies*.

Dana's Spicer Axle Division facility in Cape Girardeau, Missouri, for example, distributes a monthly bonus pool that is based on how facility-wide measures of productivity and quality compare to standard levels of performance. This money is shared among all employees (including managers) who have submitted at least two ideas that month. Each person's share is determined by how many hours he or she worked during that month, divided by the total hours worked by everyone in the facility. The philosophy of this approach is that the bonus reflects the benefits of improved performance, most of which comes about through employee ideas. At the time of our visit to this facility, the monthly bonus was adding an extra *20 percent* to most people's paychecks. It is worth noting that employees at Cape Girardeau rarely miss being eligible for this bonus. In fact, in some years they have averaged more than *double* the twenty-four ideas the company expects from them.

Boardroom uses a similar approach. It gives out substantial bonuses, which average several thousand dollars per employee per quarter, based on overall corporate performance. Because Boardroom, too, believes this performance derives largely from employee ideas, only those employees who have offered at least twenty-six ideas in that quarter are eligible for the bonus, Wainwright, with sixty-plus ideas per person per year, contributes 20 percent of its profits to employees' 401(k) plans. Each year,

[margin handwriting: Monthly bonus based on monthly productivity measures]

[margin handwriting: Must Meet Quota to get bonus]

Kacey Fine Furnitu   1uses for its
employees to perf   c areas. Top
management identu..   ε that can be
improved by employee ideas, seι⌐   each of these,
and ties specific payouts to each of the differenι ₋nilestones.

Each of the aforementioned companies has avoided the
extra costs, headaches, and behavioral dysfunction that arise
from poorly thought-out reward systems. Consequently, they get
more ideas and have far more money to share with employees.
Although each of their reward systems is different, they all follow three important principles:

1. Rewards are based on higher-level *aggregate* measures
   that reflect the *broad* and *collective* impact of everyone's
   ideas.

2. Benefits are distributed to all employees, *equitably* and
   across the board, according to transparent and publicly-
   stated rules.

3. The idea system and its reward program are *integrated*
   into the way the company is run.

Basing rewards on aggregate metrics eliminates the need to
figure out the value of every idea and who deserves the reward
for it. Overall measures also capture the benefits of small ideas
and of ideas whose benefits are intangible or difficult to measure. The financial impact of the idea at Grapevine Canyon that
increased the resort's visibility on the Internet, for example,
would be captured in the appropriate aggregate statistic, even
though its individual impact would be difficult or impossible to
determine. Because aggregate statistics capture the collective
impact of ideas, and they are derived from actual performance

instead of individual projections, they are more accurate and therefore *fairer.*

At first glance, some of the successful approaches to rewarding employee ideas may seem to be no different from standard bonus or gain-sharing programs. But there is one important difference. They are designed around ideas, which is what makes them so effective. Instead of being tactics to get people to work harder, they are strategies to help them to work smarter.

. Distributing rewards in an equitable and broad-based way creates useful synergies, because often many people are involved in taking an idea from concept through implementation. If the reward system is structured so that everyone gains from the resulting improvements, then it no longer matters (except for recognition) who originated the idea or who contributed to it along the way—everyone has an incentive to move it forward. It is in everyone's interest to support each other's ideas and to help develop and build on them. Collective reward systems also give people little incentive to manipulate the reward system for personal gain. The production manager in the electronics company discussed earlier, for example, could not have extorted money from employees because there would not have been any large rewards for him to steer in their direction. The technician's $26 million idea at the European telecommunications company would have helped the CEO, instead of making him fearful of reprisals from his board. Another benefit of spreading rewards around is that people have an incentive to share and copy ideas.

For example, at Dana, we came across one idea that, within a matter of weeks, had been copied some *fifty-six* times at one site.

To be truly effective, a reward system should be integrated into the routine of the organization. Instead of being an "add-on," it should be incorporated into the way people work and how the company is managed. The aggregate measures that drive the rewards should be derived from the company's most critical performance objectives—the same measures that drive day-to-day decision making, performance reviews, other improvement initiatives, and, ultimately, most of management's actions. This means the reward system will encourage ideas that move the organization in the direction management wants.

Let us go back to Dana's Cape Girardeau bonus system. The measures it uses are *quality*, defined as defects per million parts, and *productivity*, defined as output. These metrics balance each another, are directly tied to the primary drivers of the company's success, and are readily understood by everyone. Everyone knows how his or her specific actions—and his or her improvement ideas—affect each measure. And one of the main items on each employee's annual performance review is the quantity and quality of ideas he or she has given in.

At first glance, some of the approaches we have cited to reward employees may seem to be standard bonus or gain-sharing programs. But there is one important difference. They are designed around employee ideas, which is what makes them so effective. Instead of being tactics to get people to work harder, they are strategies to help them to work *smarter*.

A common complaint from managers about bonus and gain-sharing schemes is that they often fail to motivate employees very much. That is, the bonuses don't actually change employee behavior appreciably. At the same time, employees complain that while such schemes are a nice benefit when they do pay out, the bonuses depend mostly on factors outside their control. Many employees view bonus schemes as transparent ploys to get them to work harder. But when they are given a genuine way to have a real impact on their bonuses with ideas, the programs become much more effective.

KEY POINTS

- Seemingly commonsense reward schemes—offering a percentage of the savings or profit from each idea—can be highly counterproductive. While they seem logical and fair, they create a tremendous amount of non-value-adding work and undermine teamwork and trust.

- An organization can get all the ideas it wants *without* offering rewards. Most people already have lots of ideas, want to share them, and would be thrilled to see them used. They feel pride in their work and like to contribute to their organizations' success. For them, the best reward is to see their ideas used.

- If an organization wants to offer rewards, there are good ways to do so. The reward scheme should have three attributes:

  1. It should base the rewards on simple aggregate measurements.

  2. It should distribute rewards equitably to all employees using a fair and transparent method.

  3. It should be integrated as much as possible into how the company *already* works.

GUERRILLA TACTICS

Five actions you can take today (without the boss's permission)

1. Start with problems.   Ideas arise when someone becomes aware of a problem or opportunity. Encourage your people to identify things that make their work difficult, waste money, or detract from the customer experience and then to think of ways to fix them.

2. Identify and display problems.   Ask your people for help in identifying problems:

- Create a departmental opportunity board. Encourage everyone to post problems and opportunities on it.

- Promote an "Opportunity of the Week" or an "Opportunity of the Month." Get your people involved in identifying and selecting these opportunities.

3. Turn complaints into ideas.   When one of your people complains about something, realize that he or she may have identified a valid problem. Ask him or her for an idea to address it.

4. Follow through, follow through, follow through. Follow through on *every* idea that comes in, including those that are given to you informally. To help ensure that you don't forget about the informal suggestions, carry a notebook to record them. Remember, the best reward a person can get for an idea is to see it used.

5. Create heroes (everyone can be one).   When people come up with ideas, make sure they are recognized and given credit for them. Perhaps you might bring pizza once a month for lunch and acknowledge everyone who has made contributions.

Lunch for everyone that has contributed an idea ?

CHAPTER 4

MAKING IDEAS EVERYONE'S JOB

In 1880, the Scottish shipbuilder William Denny set up the world's first industrial suggestion system. Since that time, the suggestion box has become the method of choice for seeking employee ideas. Despite modern touches—such as collecting ideas by e-mail, Web-based applications, or special hot lines—the underlying process is the same as it was in the nineteenth century. The strange thing is that everyone knows that suggestion boxes don't work. Even cartoonists such as Scott Adams and Gary Larson poke fun at them.

Yet the suggestion box paradigm endures. In 2002, we received a call from a desperate executive at one of the largest insurance companies in the United States.

"My CEO just bought hundreds of suggestion boxes and ordered them put up throughout the company. He assigned *me* to make them work. What do I do? Every suggestion box system I have ever seen has been a total disaster."

Getting employee ideas involves a lot more than simply putting boxes on the wall. The suggestion box has fundamental limitations. It is a cumbersome and inefficient process that fails to engage employees and managers. It is premised on an archaic view of how organizations should be run, one in which employees check their brains at the door. (Some companies, as a French colleague pointed out to us, don't even think their employees *have* anything to check at the door!) The box is there on the off chance that one of them might actually have a worthwhile thought.

Our advice to that distraught insurance company executive was this: *Change the rules*. What we mean by this, and how to do it, is the subject of this chapter. It is where the idea revolution begins.

---■----------

"IT'S NOT YOUR JOB TO THINK"

At the beginning of the twentieth century, when Frederick Taylor introduced "science" into the practice of management, generally speaking he did the world a huge favor. In the first three decades after scientific management was introduced, it dramatically improved productivity almost wherever it was applied and thereby raised the standard of living around the globe. Unfortunately, Taylor saddled his new management method with a serious limitation, one that organizations still struggle with today.

This limitation was not something he *overlooked*; it was a concept he actively advocated as an essential component of his new approach to management:

All of the planning which under the old
done by the workman, as a result of h
rience, must of necessity under the ne
done by the management in accordanc
of the science. . . . It is also clear that in most cases
one type of man is needed to plan ahead and an
entirely different type to execute the work.[1]

In other words, there are those whose job is to *think* and those whose job is to *do*. Well-managed companies take control away from the front lines, even the right to question procedures.

In our scheme, we do not ask for the initiative of our
men. We do not want any initiative. All we want of
them is to obey the orders we give them, do what we
say, and do it quick.[2]

If Taylor were alive now and saying such things, he would be viewed as an embarrassment, a relic of a bygone era. One wonders how he would react if he were able to visit companies today that do not separate thinking from doing. Imagine him, for example, talking to employees at Wainwright Industries, a company in an industry that he knew well and that got sixty-five ideas per person in 2002. Taylor would recognize the lathes, the grinders, the milling and drilling machines, and the presses. But what would he be thinking as these employees showed him all the ideas they had implemented to save money and to improve productivity, quality, and safety? Wainwright has reached levels of efficiency that Taylor never even dreamed about, by doing exactly the *opposite* of what he advised.

Unfortunately, in most organizations the division between thinking and doing is "hard-wired" into policies, structures, and operating practices, although it is rarely made explicit or even recognized for what it is. To overcome a century of ingrained bad habits, something radical is clearly needed. Instead of taking thinking *out* of the job expectations for employees, why not put it explicitly *in*? And why not manage our organizations for *ideas,* instead of simply for conformance and control. That is, make *getting* ideas part of every manager's job—for supervisors, middle managers, and senior leaders. And design our policies, structures, and operating practices to *smooth* the way for ideas, rather than to *obstruct* them.

[handwritten margin note: Make getting ideas every one's job]

■

MAKING IDEAS PART OF EMPLOYEES' WORK

In 1992, Martin Edelston, CEO of Boardroom Inc., invited management guru Peter Drucker for a day of consulting. Edelston had no specific goals in mind for the day; he simply thought that Drucker might give him some interesting insights. And indeed he did. At the end of the day, Drucker reported to Edelston that many employees had told him they were frustrated by the amount of time they were wasting in unproductive meetings. Drucker made a simple suggestion. Have everyone who comes to a meeting be prepared to give an idea for making his or her work more productive or enhancing the company as a whole in some way.[3]

Edelston liked the suggestion and decided to try it. Several years later, the policy was formalized and incorporated into the weekly departmental meetings. Today, employees who fail to give in an average of at least two ideas *each week*, however small, lose their quarterly bonuses. We asked Edelston how often people missed these bonuses because they couldn't come up with enough ideas. "It hasn't happened yet," he told us.

Subsequent interviews with employees confirmed this. We were naturally a bit skeptical that for seven years every employee had produced two ideas per week without fail. With a little more digging the fuller story emerged. A lively black market had sprung up for ideas. A person who was short for a particular week would go to a coworker and borrow an idea, to be paid back at a later date. When we confronted Edelston with this discovery, we did not expect his reply. "Of course I know about this, but I think it's great. We have succeeded in creating a culture that values ideas and gets people to share and communicate them. Wasn't that the goal in the first place?"

---

*Instead of taking thinking **out** of the job expectations for employees, why not put it explicitly **in**? And why not manage our organizations for ideas, instead of simply for conformance and control? That is, make **getting** ideas part of every manager's job—for supervisors, middle managers, and senior leaders. And design policies, structures, and operating practices to **smooth** the way for ideas, rather than to **obstruct** them.*

At first encounter, Boardroom's approach seems a bold, even brassy experiment. It certainly makes ideas central to everyone's work. But is the expectation of two ideas per week unreasonably high? We asked a number of veteran Boardroom employees this question, and *not one* thought the requirement unduly harsh. In fact, they appreciated the collaborative atmosphere it created and were challenged by it. In the meetings we attended, it was obvious that people were enjoying the process of sharing and discussing ideas, as well as solving problems that affected them. Ultimately, Drucker taught Edelston something much more important than how to run effective meetings. He showed him that he could raise his expectations of his workforce.

Other organizations have made ideas part of the job in different ways. In 1991, Southwood "Woody" Morcott, CEO of Dana at the time, set a new corporate policy. From now on, every person in the company would be expected to come up with two ideas per month. According to Morcott:

> *We had to make it clear that innovation and creativity—embodied in concrete ideas—would not only be welcomed but expected.*[4]

Dana, a highly decentralized company with more than sixty thousand employees in thirty-four countries, doing everything from professional services to manufacturing, left the details of how to implement the new policy to management at the operating unit level. Each Dana unit takes its own approach. Dana's leasing operation, for example, with its salaried professional workforce, decided to begin each person's annual performance review by going over the ideas that he or she had submitted that year. The Dana Spicer Axle Division in Cape Girardeau, Missouri, opted to offer monthly bonuses to people who give in their two ideas—with the size of the bonus depending on the aggregate effect of everyone's ideas.

Milliken's expectation of 110 ideas per person per year isn't always an *individual* requirement but is sometimes written into the annual performance objectives of a *work group*. This requirement may sound stiff, but the ideas don't have to be big. For example, in the guesthouse at company headquarters, one idea was to lower the wattage of a light bulb in a supply closet. Another was to put a special hook in each room for guests to hang their garment bags on, a simple convenience that most luxury hotels lack.

Even if there is no organization-wide expectation for ideas, most managers and supervisors can create this expectation for their own employees. It can be as simple as saying, "I want you to bring an idea to each of our weekly department meetings." Most people are grateful for the chance to contribute their suggestions on how to run the organization better. And as long as the proposed changes are within the manager's domain, top management support is not an issue.

The real bottleneck to ideas is not usually front-line employees but the poor reception the ideas get from the organization. Changing this situation involves two things. First, getting employee ideas must become part of the work of *every* manager. Second, the organization itself must be aligned to *support*, rather than resist, ideas.

MAKING IDEAS PART OF THE WORK OF SUPERVISORS

In the mid-1960s, as the Vietnam War was intensifying, a lieutenant colonel put an idea into one of the Pentagon's suggestion boxes.

His office produced a constant stream of reports for senior officers, all with the same format—an executive summary, a table of contents, and thick divider sheets with protruding alphabetically ordered tabs to identify the various sections. The divider sheets came in standard packets of twenty-six, one for each letter in the alphabet. What bothered the lieutenant colonel was that because most reports had only five or six sections, only the first five or six dividers in each packet were used.

The rest were thrown away. Why not simply make the first section of each report be the letter after the one where the previous report left off, he suggested. That is, if one report used A through F, begin the next one with section G. The generals and senior officials for whom the reports were prepared would still have no trouble finding what they needed. The lieutenant colonel calculated that his idea would save the office several thousand dollars every year. He dropped it in the suggestion box and waited to see what would be done with it.

A few days later, he was brusquely summoned to the office of his commanding officer—a major general. He had no idea why he had been called in, but his boss was obviously furious. The younger officer stood stiffly at attention.

"Is this yours?" the general snapped, holding up a piece of paper that the lieutenant colonel recognized as his suggestion.

"Yes, sir."

"Eat it," the general said.

"Excuse me, sir?"

"Eat it. Now!" the general ordered. The lieutenant colonel stepped forward, took the paper from his superior, put it in his mouth, chewed it up, and swallowed it. He was abruptly dismissed and nothing more was ever said about it.

A supervisor has three important roles to play in managing ideas. The first is to create an environment that encourages them. Decades later, after that lieutenant colonel retired as one of the army's top generals, he *still* remembered the way his former superior had humiliated him that day. It was the last time that the lieutenant colonel proposed any improvements while he worked for that officer.

The second role of the supervisor is to help employees develop their knowledge and improve their problem-solving skills, in order to increase the quality and impact of their ideas. Strangely enough, the best learning opportunities often come from the *worst* ideas. Think about the lieutenant colonel's idea. Was it actually a good one? Clearly, he had identified a problem—his office was throwing out huge numbers of unused dividers. But had he come up with a good solution? Of course not. Starting reports with section K or S would seem strange. People would wonder where the missing sections were. The general could see immediately that the idea would make his command look eccentric. And rightly or wrongly, if reports didn't look professional, superiors would have less respect for their contents and would give them less weight in their decision making.

But when he rejected the suggestion in such an angry fashion, the general missed a chance to mentor his subordinate. A bad idea, given in good faith, reveals a lack of understanding on the part of the suggester. No matter how bad the idea was, the general should have seen it as a teaching opportunity. The lieutenant colonel was only trying to do his job. Had the general taken a minute or two to explain the proposal's drawbacks, the lieutenant colonel might have learned something and have become a more effective (and loyal) subordinate for it. A great many organizations spend thousands of dollars—maybe *millions* in the case of the Defense Department—on consultants or internal studies to determine training needs. But here, for no cost, the general was handed a good training opportunity.

He also lost the chance to eliminate some significant waste. The lieutenant colonel had identified a *problem*, but perhaps not a workable *solution* to it. Once he was shown *why* it was unworkable, he might have been able to come up with a different way to address the problem. Or perhaps the general could have brainstormed a bit with his aide to come up with a workable solution. Maybe the office could purchase blank dividers and type the section letters in as needed. Or perhaps section dividers could be bought packaged individually by letter, so the office could buy more A's than Z's.

But worst of all, the general's poor handling of the idea caused his subordinate to lose respect for him.

A supervisor has three important roles to play in managing ideas:

1. To create an environment that encourages ideas;

2. To help employees develop their knowledge and improve their problem solving skills, in order to increase the quality and impact of their ideas; and

3. To champion ideas and look for possible larger implications in them.

The third role a supervisor plays is to champion ideas to superiors and the rest of the organization and to look for the larger implications that can underlie even the smallest idea. Once the lieutenant colonel's idea was made workable, maybe it, or something similar, could have been used throughout the Defense Department. Or perhaps he could have thought of *other* supplies that were only being partly used. The two men might even have modified the idea and used it creatively as a visible reminder of the need to conserve resources in wartime. In short, supervisors can play an important part in unlocking the full potential in employee ideas.

Incorporating these roles into supervisors' jobs involves three things. The first is to make certain they understand why ideas are important. Many supervisors are surprised to learn of the potential for performance improvement that lies in employee ideas. Whenever we have found organizations with good idea systems tracking the sources of their performance improvement, most of it comes from employee ideas. For example, only a few years after a Johnson Controls facility in Kentucky started its idea system, the management team was already budgeting *half* the annual cost reductions it needed to come from employee ideas. At Dana, a company with a more mature system, one manager told us that his data showed *80 percent* of newly identified cost savings coming from employee ideas. Supervisors who are able to get large numbers of employee ideas find their jobs becoming much less stressful, as many problems take care of themselves and their groups become increasingly able to do more with less.

The second thing needed to make ideas central to supervisors' work is to give them training in how to manage ideas. Many of the necessary skills—such as listening, communicating, instructing, coaching, and helping people develop—are already part of an effective supervisor's repertoire. But additional training will be needed in idea-specific areas, such as how to handle bad ideas, how to get an initially reluctant employee to give in an idea, how to help employees come up with more and better ideas, how to help employees build on their ideas and develop them further, and how to ferret out the larger implications of seemingly small ideas.

The third ingredient needed to make ideas part of supervisors' jobs is to hold them accountable for how well they manage ideas, just as they are held accountable for other important aspects of their performance. This means monitoring a few statistics, such as the number of ideas each supervisor is getting from his or her employees, the participation rate, the implementation rate, and the speed of implementation. These numbers can be used in different ways to hold supervisors accountable. They might be integrated into the supervisor's normal performance reviews (as Dana does), publicized (relying on peer pressure and natural competitive instincts, as parts of Air France and Volkswagen do), made part of the criteria for promotion (as Sumitomo Electric and Toyota do), or used to recognize, celebrate, or even reward those supervisors who do well at encouraging ideas (as DUBAL does).

MAKING IDEAS PART OF THE WORK OF MIDDLE MANAGERS

From time to time, we come across idea systems in which middle managers are quietly resisting, or even outright sabotaging, perfectly good ideas. When we first encountered such behavior, we were quite puzzled by it. Why, we wondered, couldn't middle managers see the value in these ideas? And how did they attain and keep their positions of responsibility unless they cared about being effective at their jobs and moving the company forward? For a while, we simply chalked each instance up to a bad egg—a person who was uncomfortable with change and was obstructing the process. But the more we were able to identify and talk with middle managers who behaved this way, the more we began to see the issue from their perspective. The problem was not them; it was the conflicted positions their organizations put them in. It sometimes made sense for them to stonewall, simply to get their jobs done.

Consider what happened at a utility company in the northeastern United States. In the late 1990s, the industry was deregulating, and the company needed to increase its efficiency quickly to survive. A new CEO was hired to bring about the necessary change. When he took over, to familiarize himself with the company, he spent several weeks visiting its front-line operations and talking with employees. He was astonished at the number of ideas they gave him to save money and work more productively. He ordered a system to be established as a way to capture their ideas. Although plenty of ideas came in, and managers knew the CEO wanted them acted on quickly, the effort soon ran into trouble. Even the best ideas took an inordinate amount of time and effort to implement. At one point, it was taking more than a year and a half to implement the average idea.

Middle managers play a vital role in the idea process. They make sure the necessary resources are available to evaluate, test, and implement the ideas and provide the necessary training. They must also oversee the process in their units and get personally involved with the more significant ideas.

The problem turned out to be with middle managers—behind the scenes they were obstructing implementation. From their point of view, it was the safest course of action, because of a flawed policy. As soon as an idea was implemented, the projected cost savings were *immediately* deducted from the affected manager's budget. The CEO's thinking was that he or she would no longer need the funds. But managers told us privately that this policy often made it dangerous for them to approve and implement ideas. No matter how carefully the projected cost savings were calculated, they were often overestimated, sometimes grossly so. There was a natural tendency for those advocating an idea to exaggerate its value. Suggesters, who received 10 percent of the value of their ideas, would naturally give optimistic assessments of their worth; the idea system manager was anxious to show results from his program; and top management was under pressure from the board of directors to demonstrate that it was reducing costs. Also, many ideas had unanticipated complications. They cost more to implement than projected, the inevitable adjustments and minor changes needed to make them work took more time than planned, or they created unanticipated problems. Middle managers, who had to live with the difference between the stated value of ideas and their actual results, found themselves surrounded by people whose self-interest was to inflate the estimated cost savings. And even if the projected cost savings were realistic, they often did not show up until the *next* budget cycle. Unwittingly, the tight budgeting policy of that utility company made it difficult for middle managers to support employee ideas. The only way out for them was to find some excuse to turn down ideas, scale them back, or slow their implementation.

Middle managers play a vital role in the idea process. They make sure the necessary resources are available to evaluate, test, and implement ideas and to provide the necessary training. They must also oversee the process in their units and get personally involved with the more significant ideas. Yet middle managers are frequently overlooked in the way organizations set up and run their idea systems, and they get squeezed between the well-intentioned policies of top management and the day-to-day realities they face.

Once such misalignments are identified and people are made aware of them, they are often straightforward to remove. Take, for example, the problem at the New England utility. Had the CEO known about it, he could easily have set up a win-win situation. He wanted cost savings to flow more quickly to the bottom line. Middle managers are always glad to get more discretionary funds in their budgets. Why not let middle managers keep in their budgets all the savings realized from an idea for the first six months after its *approval*? Instead of resisting ideas, they would rush to get them in place as fast as possible. His middle managers would have become big fans of employee ideas.

Middle managers are in positions that are already tough enough. The last thing they need is an idea system that adds to their problems. They have to be given input into the way the idea system is run and perhaps even some autonomy to modify it so it works for their units. Once they are convinced of the value of employee ideas and given training in how to encourage, process, and implement ideas, they, too, should be held accountable for their idea-managing performance.

------ ■ ------

MAKING IDEAS PART OF THE WORK OF SENIOR LEADERS

Bruce Hertzke, CEO of Winnebago Industries, almost never travels on Fridays. Friday mornings are reserved for a special morning coffee gathering of all those who have had an idea implemented during the previous week, together with their managers. As the suggesters arrive, they are photographed with Hertzke. These photographs are published in the next issue of the company newsletter along with a brief description of each idea.

When the meeting starts, each suggester is asked to describe his or her idea and its expected results. Hertzke comments on each idea and thanks the suggester. After all the ideas have been heard, the rest of the meeting is dedicated to an open discussion of any issues that the employees or their managers want to talk about.

Leaders who are serious about promoting employee ideas have to design a role for themselves in the process. The role need not take much time, but it should keep them informed about the idea system's performance and put them in regular and personal contact with suggesters and their ideas. The leader's personal involvement has two purposes. First is the obvious need for overseeing the process and showing support for it from the top. If ideas are important to the company, the CEO has to ensure that everyone knows this and that ideas are being managed effectively. With just one hour per week, Hertzke makes it clear to both employees and managers that ideas are important to him and the company.

The second reason for the CEO's involvement is to increase his or her effectiveness. Hertzke is rare among CEOs in that he started at Winnebago as a teenager working on the assembly line. There he saw how he and his fellow workers were not listened to, though they had all kinds of ideas for improving products and processes. As a result, he is keenly aware that the nature of his job distances him from the issues and concerns of those on the front lines. For Hertzke, the Friday idea meetings are a priceless chance to stay in touch. Many leaders find it very difficult to know what is really happening in their organizations. For example, at a roundtable of business leaders we once presented to, the CEO of one of the world's largest drug companies commented that the most challenging part of his job was getting good information about what was really going on in the organization. "People tend to tell me what they think I want to hear," he said. "Sometimes I feel very out of touch."

By hearing ideas, questions, and concerns directly from his employees every week, Hertzke stays in close touch with what is going on in his company and is regularly reminded that his people are a tremendous *resource*—they care about the company, are thoughtful and observant, and often see opportunities their managers do not. Many executives are quick to lay off employees to improve financial performance. But every company we are familiar with that operates a high-performing idea system is different. *All* have designed a significant role for senior managers into their systems. The experience these managers derive from interacting with employees teaches them to view these employees not as a cost to eliminate but as a source of *help* in times of financial difficulty.

Leaders who are serious about promoting employee ideas have to design a role for themselves into the process. This role should keep them informed about the idea system's performance and put them in frequent personal contact with suggesters and their ideas. This continuously reminds them that their people are a tremendous **resource**—*they care about the company, are thoughtful and observant, and often see opportunities their managers do not.*

Take what happened at Toyota, for example, a company with a long-standing active idea system. During the 1973 oil crisis,

Japan's economy was hit severely, because the country imported almost all its oil. In less than a year, wholesale prices rose 31 percent, and consumer prices 25 percent. The automotive industry found itself in serious trouble. Gasoline prices went up by 60 percent, and the cost of some of its major raw materials rose by as much as 50 percent. Automakers were forced to raise the price of their vehicles substantially. At Toyota, sales plummeted by 37 percent.[5] Many companies faced with such a crisis would have laid people off without hesitation. Instead, Toyota asked its employees for all the cost-cutting ideas they could think of that did not require major investment. The response was immediate. Prior to the crisis, employees had been averaging two or three ideas per person per year. In 1973 this jumped to *twelve* per person—a total of 247,000 ideas corporate-wide—and it is worth noting that the call for ideas didn't go out until *October,* when the crisis began. Since 1950, Toyota has not laid a single employee off, worldwide.

Effective top management involvement in an idea system can take many different forms. At Milliken & Company, CEO Roger Milliken and President Tom Malone host quarterly idea "sharing rallies," at which the employees with the best ideas in that quarter present them to top management. Don Wainwright holds weekly recognition breakfasts for employees who have given in ideas. Every March, DUBAL, the aluminum company in Dubai, holds an annual celebration of its idea system. The one we attended in 2001 included more than two thousand company employees as well as guests from government and private sector companies. Over a hundred employees received awards for different achievements, such as "Best Supervisor" (in each of eighteen areas); "Best Suggester" (in each of eighteen areas); "Best Suggestion" (in each of eighteen areas); and first, second, and third places in a number of categories of suggestion, including energy conservation, quality, safety, and environmental.

Although CEO John Boardman personally presents each award, his main involvement occurs during the previous three months, when he leads the CEO's adjudication team, which visits all the finalists for "Best Suggestion" in their workplaces. Boardman and his team of the company's general managers listen to each suggester explain his or her idea in detail and they see it in operation.

In the course of our research and work, we have noticed a marked pattern with CEOs. When asked to share some of their favorite employee ideas, some CEOs have plenty of specific examples, but many do not. The response to this request has proven a good indicator of whether a CEO is personally involved in the idea system. If the CEO hedges, perhaps by talking vaguely about how hard it is to single out any particular idea, and quickly changes the subject, we invariably find that top-level involvement is minimal—and so are the benefits from the idea system.

MAKING IDEAS PART OF THE ORGANIZATION'S WORK

So far, we have been discussing how to make ideas a regular part of everyone's work. But doing this will have little impact unless the way the organization governs how work is done is aligned to promote ideas, too. Consider the following example.

In 2003, we helped a unit of a large medical products company to launch a new idea system. The vice president in charge of the unit had formed a team to design the process. Members of the team had worked hard, done their jobs well, and even proposed ways to make ideas part of everyone's work. Unfortunately, the organization itself was not ready for employee ideas.

One problem was that front-line supervisors were spread very thin. In some cases, a single supervisor had *fifty* direct reports. Moreover, many supervisors had to spend literally *half* of their time in meetings and were constantly blindsided by urgent tasks from above. A number of supervisors estimated that they were able to spend *at most* 20 percent of their time actually supervising. At the same time, front-line employees complained that it was extremely difficult for them to get any attention from their supervisors. No matter what the team designing the process added to supervisors' job descriptions, how could supervisors really be expected to fit anything more into their hectic schedules?

Making ideas a regular part of everyone's work will have little impact unless the way the organization governs how work is done is aligned to promote ideas, too. The best idea systems are so completely integrated into the way the organization operates that they are indistinguishable from other systems and processes.

Front-line employees had a similar problem. The accounting system was set up to allocate their time to the production of specific products. There was no way to allocate time for them to meet and talk about ideas, let alone help implement them.

Figure 4.1 The alignment ladder

Many additional misalignments were identified. Supervisors and managers faced conflicting performance metrics; budgets were so tightly controlled that it would be difficult to get the resources to implement many ideas; everyone complained of poor vertical communication and communication between shifts. Even ideas with no impact on product integrity had to go through engineering review. It was clear to us that in order to make the new idea system a success, managers were going to have to realign the organization to handle employee ideas.

A handy conceptual tool for thinking about alignment is the ladder shown in figure 4.1. Its logic is as follows. An organization faces a certain external *environment*. The *strategy* it follows must successfully draw needed resources from that environment. The organization's *structure* should be designed to support the strategy, as should the *policies* it follows and the way it *budgets* its resources. The *systems* and *procedures* it deploys, in turn, should be consistent with its strategy, structure, budgets, and policies. Smoothly meshing with all of this are the way people are *rewarded*, the *skills* they are given through training, and the way they are *supervised*. The ultimate goal is to assure that throughout the organization, individual *behavior*—in this case submitting and managing ideas—is in line with the organization's strategic direction. The role played by the organization's *culture* and its *leadership* is to keep all these elements aligned. Resistance to ideas will arise when any of these elements are out of step with managing employee ideas, and mixed messages will be sent to people who have been told that generating and working with ideas are critical parts of their jobs.

Misalignments manifest themselves in many ways. Earlier, in the section about middle managers, we discussed how an electric utility put its managers in a difficult position when company policies inadvertently conflicted with implementing ideas. This was a fairly obvious example of misalignment because it resulted in *already-approved* ideas being blocked. In most cases, poor alignment is more subtle. It merely causes some aspect of the idea system to underperform—people may not step forward with as many ideas, processing might take longer, and some areas of the organization could resist ideas from other areas. However misalignments happen, they make it more difficult for people truly to embrace working with ideas as a normal part of their job.

The best idea systems are so completely integrated into the way the organization operates that they are indistinguishable from other systems and processes. Working with ideas is simply part of the way everything is done.

KEY POINTS

- Traditional management practice is to take thinking *out* of the jobs of front-line employees. Best-practice companies put it explicitly in. Employees are expected to come up with ideas as part of their normal work.

- A supervisor has three important roles to play when it comes to managing ideas: (1) to create a supportive environment; (2) to coach, mentor, and develop subordinates' skills in coming up with ideas (the best learning opportunities often come from the worst ideas); and (3) to help flesh out and properly develop employee ideas, champion them, and look for their larger implications.

- The middle manager's job is to promote ideas in his or her area, assure resources are available for training and implementation, and become personally involved with more substantial ideas that require his or her attention. To assure that middle managers are not put in conflicted positions, top management has to eliminate any misalignments in policies or practices that send inconsistent messages.

- Leaders should be personally involved in the idea system for two reasons: to champion it and oversee its performance and to increase their personal effectiveness. Regular contact with front-line employees reminds them that employees are a tremendous resource—thoughtful and observant people who often see things their managers don't.

- The way the organization governs how work is done should be aligned to promote ideas. The best idea systems are extremely well integrated into the way the organization operates.

GUERRILLA TACTICS

Five actions you can take today (without the boss's permission)

1. Make ideas a priority for everyone.   Make consideration and discussion of ideas the *first* item in your regular department meetings. Incorporate ideas into the annual performance review process. Assess how well each person does at coming up with or encouraging ideas. Talk about how he or she might improve, and identify training and development opportunities.

2. Publicize results.   Track the number of ideas people are submitting. For supervisors and managers, track the number of ideas they are *getting.* Post the results.

3. Address bottlenecks.   If it takes too long to process ideas, find out why. Are people sitting on ideas for good reasons? Is the problem caused by a misalignment? Ask people about unintended consequences of policies or practices that are getting in the way of dealing with ideas.

4. Exploit learning opportunities.   When someone suggests a bad idea, treat it as a learning opportunity. Why did that person think it made sense? What information, knowledge, or training do you need to provide to that person?

(continued)

5. Recruit your boss.   Life will be a lot easier if your boss is supportive. Start a campaign to regularly bring great ideas to his or her attention. It may require subtlety, but when constantly confronted with ideas that your people have offered and that have helped achieve goals and have improved performance, he or she should eventually come around.

CHAPTER 5

PUTTING THE PROCESS IN PLACE

This chapter lays out the characteristics of a good idea system. Without some kind of systematic approach, it would be impossible, even with the best of intentions, to deal with large numbers of ideas. What we mean by an "idea system" is a set of procedures—whether for a small group or an entire organization—that ensures that employee ideas are handled smoothly and fairly.

In our experience, many managers believe that structure and formality hamper the free flow of ideas. When they are shown the data from high-performing idea systems, a typical reaction goes something like this:

> *The only difference between these companies and mine is that they have a formal process for tracking ideas, and we don't. In my company, all this happens naturally. The paperwork and record*

*keeping would just get in the way. Every manager
here knows it's important to listen to ideas, and our
employees feel perfectly comfortable approaching us.
We all have open-door policies. We have more of a
"family" approach.*

Perhaps in an ideal world or on a small entrepreneurial team, ideas could be managed this way. Tellingly, however, these same managers are not as casual about other things. Take travel expenses, for example. Would these managers leave a big barrel of cash in the corner and tell employees who are traveling to take whatever they need, spend it wisely, and put back whatever they don't use? No need for receipts or a report, because they just get in the way, and "we're just one big happy family?"

No organization manages its money this way, because it would soon be out of business. It has to ensure that what is *supposed* to be happening *is* actually happening. And, of course, managers who claim—in the absence of any measurement or control mechanisms—that large numbers of ideas in their organizations are naturally flowing to welcoming supervisors and being quickly implemented, are deluding themselves.

For one thing, the absence of a system makes employee ideas more of a nuisance than a help. Every idea that comes up has to be handled in an ad hoc manner. Not only does the employee involved have to figure out who to take it to, but that person also has to figure out what to do with it. Because every idea is handled differently, ideas require more time and effort to deal with. Managers who advocate completely informal idea processes often do not realize how these actually *discourage* people from bringing up ideas. A smoothly running system that is well integrated into the organization's daily routine takes the hassle out of dealing with ideas and makes it feasible and reasonable for ideas to become central to everyone's work.

While every organization should design its process according to its unique needs, certain characteristics are common to all high-performing idea systems:

1. Ideas are encouraged and welcomed.

2. Submitting ideas is simple.

3. Evaluation of ideas is quick and effective.

4. Feedback is timely, constructive, and informative.

5. Implementation is rapid and smooth.

6. Ideas are reviewed for additional potential.

7. People are recognized, and success is celebrated.

8. Idea system performance is measured, reviewed, and improved.

CHARACTERISTIC 1: IDEAS ARE ENCOURAGED AND WELCOMED

The most effective encouragement an organization can give its employees to step forward with ideas is a track record of using ideas and giving people credit for them. Building this record can be a challenge, particularly if management has a long history of being unresponsive. Employees may have learned from experience that despite management rhetoric, in reality their ideas are far more likely to get them in trouble than to win them praise. To get people participating, managers may have to make special efforts to encourage ideas and demonstrate that they will be taken seriously. In particular, they must treat the first tentative suggestions of every employee very carefully.

Consider what happened at Milliken Denmark when a janitor came up with an idea that put management in an awkward position. One of his jobs was to maintain the area in front of the entrance to the main building. He had noticed that visitors would often arrive late and flustered because they had had trouble finding the facility. (We had the same difficulty—our taxi driver took several wrong turns, had to stop a number of times to look at the map and we, too, arrived late.) The janitor's idea was this: Buy a huge balloon and float it high above the facility to make it easy for people to find.

It didn't take long for management to realize that this idea was quite impractical, given the expense and the strong winds along the northern Danish coast. But there was a problem: The janitor had just joined the company. This was his *first* idea, and management wanted to bend over backward to accept it. No one could find a way to make it work, but no one wanted to let the employee down, either. After wrestling with it for several weeks, senior management finally hit on a way out: Tell him a white lie. It was a wonderful idea, the employee was told. The management team had really liked it. Unfortunately, the Danish aviation authorities (who, in truth, had never been contacted) had told the company that the balloon would be illegal for safety reasons. The facility was too close to the Aarhus International Airport (it was in fact over thirty kilometers away), and if the balloon were ever to break loose, it might meander into the path of an airliner. The ploy worked, and the employee never found out about the fib. Over the years that followed, he went on to suggest a great many good ideas.

However managers do it, they have to make it clear to everyone that each idea will be taken seriously. One effective tactic is to make a tangible commitment of personal involvement. For example, at a national marketing company, a single department manager decided to implement an idea system in his area. He personally chaired the biweekly meeting to discuss ideas and took responsibility for following through on many of them. This sent a strong signal to his staff. When Boardroom CEO Martin Edelston launched his company's idea initiative, for more than a year, every idea from his approximately fifty employees went directly to him. He personally evaluated each one, gave his reaction to it, and followed through when necessary to see that it was implemented. When American Airlines started up its idea system, CEO Robert Crandall put in place a tough policy. Every idea that was not acted on within 150 days—an appropriate time for the airline industry—was automatically forwarded to him. Word quickly spread among managers that it was not pleasant to be called to his office and be asked to explain why they had been sitting on a potentially valuable idea.

Such unambiguous and visible management commitment makes it clear to employees that their ideas will be welcomed and that managers who *don't* welcome them are out of step with their leaders. But even with this commitment, sometimes a more direct and personal nudge is needed to get a person to step forward with ideas. In the early years of American's system, one suggestion came in to improve the system itself. Since it was generally perceived as a "headquarters" program, the suggester pointed out, why not put representatives out at the field stations who could actively promote the system to employees?

The idea was adopted, and the "IdeAAdvocates" program was created. Every year, each station would nominate a person as its IdeAAdvocate. He or she would attend a day-long training session in Dallas, to learn about the program and how to encourage fellow employees to submit ideas. Within a year of the start of this company-wide program of personal encouragement, the number of employee ideas *doubled.*

Top managers can also give impetus to an idea system *indirectly.* A few years before the janitor's balloon suggestion, Milliken Denmark's idea program had been languishing, and the company had decided to revitalize it. The managing director came up with a subtle and imaginative approach to break the ice and get things started. He sent his administrative assistant around to ask people individually whether they had any thoughts on how to improve things. She was a good choice of emissary. She was generally liked and respected, and she was threatening to no one. Nevertheless, her status as the boss's assistant made people take her seriously. As employees gave her their ideas, she filled out slips for them and put them into the system. Soon employees began getting thank-you notes and seeing their ideas acted on. Over time, she began asking people with suggestions to fill the slips out *themselves.* Ultimately, the system became one of the benchmark idea systems in Europe.

CHARACTERISTIC 2: SUBMITTING IDEAS IS SIMPLE

Many organizations that want employee ideas unwittingly make it difficult for people to submit them. They gear their processes for the biggest and most complex ideas that might come along. The suggestion forms ask for reams of information, copies of the forms are distributed to everyone who might possibly need to engage with the idea, and numerous signatures are required for approval. But the vast majority of front-line ideas are modest and straightforward to implement. A long and complicated form sends a not-very-subtle message that the only ideas of interest are significant ones. Who would send in an idea to lower the wattage of a light bulb in a particular supply closet (as one Milliken employee did) on a multipage form destined for review by several layers of management? At one large German company we advised, we estimated that *three-quarters* of the information requested on the form was superfluous for most ideas, and two of the copies were *never* used. The key is to design the submission process to match the kinds of ideas that employees will come up with—that is, mostly small ones. Should more information be needed, the employee can always be asked for it.

With this in mind, the process of submitting an idea can be made extremely simple. At Boardroom, all ideas are submitted on pieces of paper the size of a business card. Wainwright Industries uses three-by-five yellow slips of paper. Milliken and Idemitsu Kosan use full-size sheets of paper designed for multiple ideas. Some divisions of Dana and Dresser Industries ask employees to write their suggestions on special cards and post them on idea boards. LaSalle Bank and units of ABB collect ideas online with all suggester contact information filled in automatically by the computer. The few ideas that are too big or complex to capture this way are handled as exceptions and bumped into more elaborate processes.

Another aspect of making it simple to submit ideas is to provide people with the support and access to information they need to develop more complex ideas. Think back to Art Sampson's idea at the Defense Finance and Accounting Service (discussed in chapter 3). After conceiving the idea, he had to quantify how much time his organization was wasting dealing with missing checks. He had to learn about the Treasury's system for tracking cashed checks, find out how his department might get permission to use this system, and figure out the details of the improved missing check procedure. Finally, he had to make the case for his proposal to management. In other words, he needed *access* to appropriate information and expertise, *time* to work on his idea, and the ability to *test* its feasibility.

The process of submitting an idea can be made extremely simple. The key is to design it to match the kinds of ideas that employees will come up with— mostly small ones. Should more information be needed, the suggester can always be asked for it.

Supervisors have tremendous leverage over the quantity and quality of employee ideas through the role they play in getting their people the support needed to develop ideas. In the late 1990s, an assembly line worker at Volvo's Gothenberg plant stunned engineers with the largest idea in the history of the company's suggestion system. His idea was to use advances in computerized fuel injection systems to control the fuel–air mix precisely enough so that certain pollution control equipment in each car's exhaust system could be eliminated. With his supervisor's help, the worker borrowed a vehicle to experiment with and got permission to use the maintenance shop and equipment on evenings and weekends. When he submitted his idea, engineers rejected it as laughably impossible. Imagine their surprise when he rolled out a fully functioning test vehicle! The idea saved Volvo millions of dollars.

———■———————

CHARACTERISTIC 3: EVALUATION OF IDEAS IS QUICK AND EFFECTIVE

As mentioned earlier, when Boardroom's Martin Edelston started his company's idea system, he evaluated every employee idea personally. With fifty employees turning in two ideas per week, this meant he had to make decisions about a *hundred* ideas each week. His routine was to do this on the weekend while riding his exercise bike. (The resulting long workouts made him fitter than he had been in a long time, he told us.) One Sunday, he read a proposal from a programmer for a software improvement that he couldn't understand. On Monday, he stopped by the man's office and asked him to explain it. After half an hour, Edelston still didn't understand it. And then came an epiphany.

Edelston had hired this employee—a professional programmer—for his expertise. He understood far more about the company's computer system than Edelston ever would. Why, then, was *Edelston* the one trying to decide whether the software change made sense or not? He realized that decisions about ideas were best made by those most familiar with the situation involved. His personal involvement with every idea might have been needed to get his system started, but now he was only getting in the way.

Today, most decisions about ideas at Boardroom are made on the spot in the weekly department meetings. Relatively few are passed up the chain of command. Edelston had discovered a key principle: Making decisions about ideas at the lowest possible level in the organization leads to *better* decisions and *faster* implementation, and frees managers to focus on what they should be focusing on.

Most ideas are relatively small, and to appreciate them a person must have specific knowledge of the local circumstances. This knowledge usually resides in the same place that the ideas were formulated. The more managers remove routine decision making about ideas from employees, the more it slows things down, and the higher the probability that the decisions will be poor ones.

---

*Making decisions about ideas at the lowest possible level in the organization leads to **better** decisions and **faster** implementation, and frees managers to focus on what they should be focusing on.*

Although it is not uncommon for remote decision making to cause bad ideas to be approved, it generally skews the evaluation process in the opposite direction, making it overly cautious and prone to rejection. The less knowledge a person has of the context of an idea, the more information he or she needs to approve it. Approving an idea means taking some responsibility for the change involved. Rejecting it, on the other hand, merely maintains the status quo, and few people ever get in trouble for that. And the more distant a person is from the problem or opportunity that prompted the idea, the less urgently he or she feels the need for the proposed change. All this explains why the further away decisions are made from their point of impact, the longer they take, the more paperwork they generate, the costlier they are to make, and the worse they tend to be.

Evaluating ideas at the lowest possible level is what underlies the astonishing speed with which some organizations can respond to them. Milliken, for example, has a "24/72" policy: Every idea is acknowledged within twenty-four hours, and a decision about it is made within seventy-two hours. (The decision might be to initiate further study.)

Ideally, the suggesters themselves should make as many decisions as possible about their own ideas. At Dana, for example, it is corporate policy that every employee is the company's top expert in the twenty-five square feet he or she works in and should be the one deciding about ideas there. Employees have the authority to spend up to $50 on an improvement without the approval of management. Toyota and Wainwright also emphasize action rather than ideas. They don't expect most ideas to be reported to the formal system until *after* they are implemented.

However much decision-making authority is pushed down to the front lines, some ideas will still require the attention of management or of people in other departments. Art Samson at DFAS could not have made the decision alone to change the procedure for lost checks. He needed to interact with several other functions and the Treasury Department and required the active support of upper management. And sometimes cross-functional ideas, or those requiring significant investment, may justify special ad hoc teams to work them through. But all these types of ideas are exceptions, and should be treated as such, when determining what the process for handling ideas will be.

■
——————

CHARACTERISTIC 4: FEEDBACK IS TIMELY, CONSTRUCTIVE, AND INFORMATIVE

When people know the status of their ideas and get timely and informative feedback, it helps maintain their ownership and interest in the ideas as well as their trust in the process. Good feedback demonstrates that an idea was taken seriously, even if it was rejected. Perhaps it was unworkable because the employee didn't understand something or lacked a critical piece of information. Or maybe the idea was not fully understood by those considering it, because either it was poorly presented or they didn't understand the issues involved. Good feedback gives the employee a chance to refine the idea or champion it better.

Feedback need not be extensive, nor does it have to take much time. For most ideas, it can be given on the spot and orally. At Boardroom and Grapevine Canyon, for example, ideas are presented by employees in their team or department meetings. Feedback is immediate as the group discusses the idea, refines or builds on it, discovers problems with it, and decides on what to do with it. Other companies, such as Dana Hopkinsville and Dresser Industries, give feedback on their idea boards, where everyone can learn from it. LaSalle Bank's Web-based system allows employees to check on the status of their ideas at any time and read evaluators' comments.

In summary, feedback plays four important roles. It keeps the suggester engaged, is a targeted training tool, provides a check on the evaluators, and creates a dialogue that enables suggesters to tinker with their ideas and make them work.

CHARACTERISTIC 5: IMPLEMENTATION IS RAPID AND SMOOTH

To achieve rapid and efficient implementation of ideas, managers have to assure that the right resources are available to handle the volume and types of ideas that will come in. But until an organization has some experience with the flow of its employee ideas, it is difficult to predict what the required profile of resources will be.

To understand this point better, consider what we have come to call the "surge problem." This phenomenon often occurs when an organization starts up an idea system after years of giving employees no place to go with the problems and opportunities they see. No matter how efficient the idea process is, in the beginning it is completely overwhelmed.

In the mid-1990s, a large New England retailer and clothes maker started up an idea system. Management was trying to get into the highly competitive business of selling military uniforms. It wanted employee ideas to help trim costs and improve quality. A pilot idea system was started in a department that had long been a poor performer.

When the management team was warned that since the department had so many problems, it should prepare for a substantial surge in ideas, the CEO remarked, "My employees haven't given in a single idea for more than a century. What makes you think they are suddenly going to start producing large numbers of them now?" Wanting to keep tight control over the process, the CEO assigned the vice president of operations responsibility for personally responding to every idea and making certain it was implemented.

Within two weeks, the thirty members of the department had submitted some 130 ideas. The poor vice president was hopelessly overloaded. A rule of thumb for the centralized suggestion box–type system this company had insisted on is that it takes about four hours of management or staff time to process each idea. In other words, this vice president had just been handed more than *five hundred* hours of extra work. Quite reasonably, he thought an organization-wide system like this involving several *thousand* employees would be impossible to handle. And so, after only a handful of suggestions had been implemented, he saw to it that the idea system was quietly killed.

The clothes maker's attempt failed because it was not prepared for the overwhelming eagerness with which its employees responded. With its cumbersome process and lack of resources, its system simply collapsed.

Consider, on the other hand, what happened when BIC Corporation launched its idea system in the mid-1990s. Again, the early burst of ideas was a surprise to its management. Many of the suggestions required maintenance and engineering time, but developing and implementing employee ideas was a low priority for these two departments. A huge backlog of unimplemented ideas quickly developed. Charlie Tichy, the union cocoordinator of the new program, came to Manufacturing Manager Dick Williams with the problem and the solution for it. Every Friday, a dedicated implementation team—which included an electrician, a millwright, and a toolmaker—was charged with implementing the suggestions.

To achieve rapid and efficient implementation, managers have to align the resources available for implementation with the volume and types of ideas that come in. Delays in implementation cost money. Astonishingly, many managers who are desperate to find cost savings or additional revenue overlook this obvious source of funds.

BIC's response illustrates the type of creativity and flexibility that is sometimes needed to align resources to the volume and types of ideas that come in. When the bottlenecks in maintenance and engineering developed, alert managers responded rapidly. In our experience, companies that have trouble with implementation often lack the flexibility or willingness to redeploy resources to their bottlenecks. Typically, they are running lean, have tight budgeting, or are dealing with turf issues that make it difficult to share personnel. Whatever the reason, their ability to implement suffers, and employees lose trust in management's sincerity.

As an organization gains experience with employee ideas, patterns emerge in the resources needed. At BIC, many ideas required help from the maintenance and engineering departments. In other organizations, it will be different. Information technology (IT) capacity, for example, is a frequent bottleneck. At one federal government agency we worked with, the average backlog for software change requests was *three years*. Despite the obvious need for more IT resources, the agency failed to provide them. The message to its seventeen thousand employees was clear: Don't bother giving in any ideas that involve software changes.

Contrast this with a Canadian company we evaluated for a quality award. Because many improvement ideas involved software changes, it set up a special rapid-response team. Its processing became so fast that turnaround times were tracked in *minutes.*

Delays in implementation cost money. But since this money is an opportunity cost, rather than a specific expense or loss of expected income, it does not show up on financial reports and often goes unnoticed. It is astonishing how many organizations in fiercely competitive situations, whose managements are desperate to find cost savings or additional revenues, overlook this obvious source of funds. Remember the New England utility from chapter 4 that was facing deregulation? Its management was under considerable pressure to find efficiencies, yet it had an eighteen-month backlog of unimplemented ideas worth almost $2 million a year in unrealized savings. But this number did not reflect the *real* cost of the backlog. What about all the ideas that employees *didn't* submit because they didn't think the company was serious about wanting them?

As we have already discussed, the vast majority of ideas are small, simple, and straightforward to implement. Just as the evaluation process works better when decisions are made at the lowest possible levels, the implementation process works better when the authority to act on ideas is pushed down to the front lines. We mentioned earlier that at Dana every employee is authorized to spend up to $50 to implement an idea. But some Dana divisions authorize $500, as long as the employee's work team approves the idea. Front-line supervisors can generally make capital spending decisions up to $10,000 on their own.[1] When we asked one Dana plant manager how well such policies worked in practice—that is, were these policies ever abused, or was there ever a problem with unbudgeted expenditures?—he laughed. He told us that his front-line workers had proven far more conservative and resourceful with spending decisions than his managers had. And as far as unbudgeted spending was concerned, most of the ideas had such rapid paybacks that they paid for themselves within the same budget cycle. In other words, rapid implementation not only keeps the ideas coming in but delivers the savings or additional revenue from them quickly to the bottom line.

CHARACTERISTIC 6: IDEAS ARE REVIEWED FOR ADDITIONAL POTENTIAL

In several places in this book, we discuss how ideas can lead to further ideas. The sixth characteristic of a good idea system is that it incorporates post-implementation processing to exploit these opportunities.

Organizations are integrated systems, with many interrelated components. As such, even a minor change in one place can create the need for adjustments in other places—that is, for more ideas. Take Harald's idea at Grapevine Canyon Ranch that we described in chapter 2: "I can translate ride and brochure information into German." Once this is done, still more changes will have to be made. How will the German guests learn about the translations? Perhaps the brochure rack in the reception area will need additional pockets, or the Web site might need to have a German option. Or maybe the reservations computer should alert the front desk when German guests are coming, so that when they check in, the documents can be waiting for them.

It is important that every idea be looked at to see whether it creates further problems or opportunities. While the idea system itself should ultimately pick up most of these, many can be discovered more rapidly by considering the broader impact of ideas as they come in.

In chapter 2, we also discussed how small ideas can often lead to much bigger ones, if the right questions are asked. The obvious first question is "Where else can this idea be used?" If it can be used elsewhere, then the next move is to get it to those places. If employees are generally aware of the principle of replication, ideas will naturally spread inside the immediate work units to wherever they can be used, as employees learn of each other's ideas. But an extra step in the process is often needed to move ideas *outside* the work unit, to other units, functions, or locations. The simpler this process, the more effective it is. There are two strategies for replicating ideas. To use an analogy from manufacturing, one is a *push* process, in which ideas are sent to people elsewhere in the organization who may be able to use them. The other is a *pull* process, which helps people to find ideas that might be useful to them. Here are some of the different approaches companies have used:

- Determine who can use the idea, and send it to that person. At Abela, the multinational catering company headquartered in the United Arab Emirates, whenever an idea comes in at one site that might be useful at others, its director is expected to write to his or her counterparts about it.

- Use the company newsletter. At Idemitsu Kosan, broadly replicable ideas are published in a special column in the monthly *Kaizen* newsletter.

- Create a database of replicable ideas. Under the Adopt an IdeAA program, an American Airlines employee who found an idea in the airline's idea database that could be used at his or her station got a reward of $50 for implementing it there.

- Give people credit for replicating ideas. At some Dana facilities, copying an idea is as good as originating one, as far as the company's two-ideas-per-month expectation is concerned.

- Create forums to share replicable ideas. At Milliken, facility managers meet regularly, and one of the standing items on the agenda is to share replicable employee ideas.

The final aspect of leveraging ideas for additional opportunities is to make sure that people know that a single idea, or a pattern of ideas, may be piecemeal responses to a much larger issue. The power of an idea system increases exponentially with the broad-based ability to spot the larger issues that small ideas point to. Instead of nibbling away pieces of problems with ad hoc ideas, the organization gains the ability to address their root causes *systematically.*

---■---------

CHARACTERISTIC 7: PEOPLE ARE RECOGNIZED, AND SUCCESS IS CELEBRATED

Few people would argue against the importance of recognizing people for their ideas. But recognition can be tricky, and there is considerable controversy about the best way to do it. Hundreds of books and thousands of articles have been written on the topic, and consultants and recognition professionals abound. Nevertheless, a great many recognition schemes end up inspiring more cynicism than motivation. Recognition is so situation- and person-specific that it is hard to run controlled experiments to find out what really works and what doesn't. Lunch with the CEO may be a real pleasure for one person but torture for someone else. Should recognition be based on extrinsic or intrinsic motivation? Is it more effective to give it to individuals or to groups? Experts disagree.

Fortunately, when it comes to recognizing ideas, the picture is much clearer. As discussed in chapter 3, the reason people offer ideas is that they want to see them used. They feel pride in their work and enjoy contributing to the organization's success. This means that the single most effective form of recognition for ideas is to *use them*. Every implemented idea shows employees that their contributions are appreciated and that they themselves matter to the organization. And when the idea is implemented, it solves the problem or takes advantage of the opportunity that prompted it in the first place.

It is also important to credit people for their ideas. At the DCM-Toyota facility near Delhi, India, for example, the only explicit form of recognition for ideas was a bright red sticker attached to a place where each idea applied. The sticker gave the name of the person who originated the idea and a brief description of it. The offices and assembly line were festooned with them. This was a clever recognition double whammy. Not only did this remind employees that their ideas were valued, but the sheer numbers of stickers reminded them on a daily basis that ideas were a real priority for their managers.

This is not to say that additional forms of recognition cannot add something. They can make the idea process more lively, fun, and interesting, and reiterate the organization's gratitude for each idea. This is why some companies give small gifts to people, such as T-shirts, pens, mugs, or key chains. The purpose is not to reward them but to *thank* them.

Other companies create opportunities to celebrate ideas. Wainwright has a weekly bagel breakfast for its suggesters. Every employee who has given in an idea during the previous week is invited and is given a ticket for a drawing with a $50 cash prize. He or she is also entered into a monthly lottery with a $250 prize and a quarterly one with a $1,000 prize. Similarly, Dana Hopkinsville holds a lottery at its monthly employee meeting, but the prizes are a little different. The winners come up on stage and spin a prize wheel—with prizes ranging from sweatshirts to preferred parking places and even paid days off. The nice thing about a lottery is that it is easy to administer, generates a lot of excitement for relatively little cost, and *everyone* who submits an idea participates in it.

The most effective form of recognition for ideas is to use them and give people credit for them.

The more personal and sincere the recognition, the more it reminds people that they are an important part of the team and that their contributions are valued. Winnebago Industries' Friday morning gatherings (described in chapter 4), in which CEO Bruce Hertzke listens to ideas and thanks the employees involved for them, is a good example of this approach. Because he started out at Winnebago working on the assembly lines and clearly respects front-line employees, they value his praise and attention. The same approach might not work for another

CEO—especially one who lacks the same bond with his or her people. Every leader must find an approach that matches his or her situation and personality. DUBAL CEO John Boardman has designed a recognition process that fits his style. Recall that every year, his company has an annual celebration in which many employees are recognized for their involvement in the idea system. Boardman leads the team of general managers that selects the *overall* best ideas of the year. It visits the workplaces of nominees from some twenty departments, listens to a presentation about each idea, and sees it in operation. The personal attention that senior managers give to large numbers of employees and their supervisors during this evaluation process is a solid recognition mechanism in its own right.

Personal recognition does not have to come only from the top. Recognition from peers and immediate supervisors is just as powerful and helps build camaraderie. It, too, can be designed into the process. Boardroom's approach—that is, the discussion of ideas at team or department meetings—provides constant reinforcement of this kind, in that it involves peers and supervisors in appreciating, evaluating, building on, and implementing ideas.

DUBAL has an interesting way to involve supervisors in the idea process. Employees give their ideas directly to their supervisors, who are allowed to give rewards up to the equivalent of about $25. To get a larger amount for an idea, the supervisor must champion it at a weekly meeting of all supervisors. This committee can approve rewards up to $125 or so. (Note that the "rewards" are kept low enough so as not to create any of the dysfunction described in chapter 3.) This process serves two purposes. First, when a supervisor publicly advocates an employee's idea, it is a potent form of recognition. Second, it brings the more significant ideas to the attention of all supervisors, who might be able to use some of them in their own departments.

———■———

CHARACTERISTIC 8: IDEA SYSTEM PERFORMANCE IS MEASURED, REVIEWED, AND IMPROVED

As with any core processes, managers must be able to monitor the performance of their idea system and continually identify opportunities to improve it. The metrics necessary to do this at a basic level track three things: the quantity of ideas, where they come from, and the speed at which they are processed.

Quantity metrics measure the average number of ideas per employee over a given time period, whether a week, month, quarter, or year. This number is the primary indicator of how well the company is managing ideas and, since it is the most common statistic kept by companies, provides an easy benchmark to compare performance and to guide overall improvement efforts. Tracking a quantity measure over time also helps an organization develop a deeper understanding of the causes of the ebbs and flows in idea activity. These may arise because of seasonalities in business activity or may be driven by specific events. For example, many companies experience a spike in the number of ideas immediately after major change takes place—such as a new product or service launch, a reengineering initiative, a restructuring, or the installation of a new computer system. Knowing the causes of increases and declines in the number of ideas allows managers to do better at allocating the necessary resources to handle them.

Frequent charting of quantity metrics also acts as an excellent early warning system. Unexpected jumps or drops in idea activity usually have a cause. When ideas dry up, something may be causing morale problems or otherwise deterring employee involvement. Whatever the reason, it needs to be investigated and responded to quickly.

Source metrics measure *where* ideas are coming from. The most common of these metrics is the *participation rate*—that is, the percentage of people in a given unit, or the company as a whole, who give in ideas during a particular time period, typically a quarter or a year. This metric identifies gaps in deployment or coverage of the system. In 2000, we conducted research in a well-known Swedish company that, based on a high average number of ideas per employee, had been recognized for having one of the best suggestion systems in the country. Interestingly, 85 percent of the ideas in this six hundred–person company came from only *three* employees, who all reported to the same supervisor. In other words, while the quantity metrics (the criteria used in the national rankings) may have looked good for this idea system, it was hardly an example for the rest of the country to emulate. Had the company tracked participation by department, it would have identified the problem, and instead of looking at the idea system with pride, top management might have asked the question it should have been asking: What was that one supervisor doing that the others were not?

Data on where ideas are coming from allow an organization to discover all kinds of important facts about its system. In the mid-1990s, for example, an internal study at American Airlines revealed that more than half of the cost savings from ideas came from the *11* percent of them submitted by two or more people.

The reason, it turned out, was that team ideas tended to tackle more substantial issues and to be better worked out. Immediately, management initiated efforts to encourage more team ideas. As we mentioned in chapter 2, without source data, Swedish companies might never have discovered an unwitting bias in the national labor contracts' rules governing idea systems that was causing women to give in suggestions at only 10 percent of the rate of men.

Velocity metrics track a company's *responsiveness* to ideas. How long does it take to make decisions about them? How fast are people getting feedback about their suggestions? How quickly are ideas implemented? As discussed earlier, responsiveness is important for getting people to participate. Moreover, the faster a company evaluates and implements ideas, the sooner it will reap the benefits, and the lower its processing costs will be. Speed does not come from allocating massive resources to evaluation and implementation. It comes from an efficient process. Milliken would find it impossible to maintain its 24/72 response rule with a poor process. By tracking the time it takes ideas to move through each stage of the process, bottlenecks are quickly identified and targeted for improvement or elimination.

With just a handful of metrics, managers can have a good sense of how their idea system is operating, and where it can be improved.

KEY POINTS

An effective idea process has eight key characteristics:

- **Ideas are encouraged and welcomed.** The best way to encourage ideas is to be responsive to them. The challenge in the beginning is to get employees to believe managers truly want their ideas.

- **Submitting ideas is simple.** Many processes are geared for the biggest and most complex ideas that might come along. An efficient process targets *small* ideas and treats the bigger proposals as exceptions.

- **Evaluation of ideas is quick and effective.** Pushing decision making down to the front lines for as many ideas as possible leads to *better* decisions, *faster* implementation, and *lower* processing costs, and frees up managers' time.

- **Feedback is timely, constructive, and informative.** This keeps employees engaged in the process, demonstrates that their ideas are taken seriously, and promotes learning. If the idea was rejected or misunderstood, feedback allows people to find ways to improve it or to communicate it better.

- **Implementation is rapid and smooth.** Quick implementation results in more ideas and faster realization of their benefits. To handle large numbers of small ideas efficiently, an organization has to provide resources that can be easily tapped by front-line employees.

- **Ideas are reviewed for additional potential.** The power of an idea system increases exponentially with the ability to spot the larger issues that small ideas point to. Instead of nibbling away at problems, the organization can now systematically address their root causes.

- **People are recognized, and success is celebrated.** The most effective form of recognition for ideas is to implement them rapidly and to give credit to the employees involved.

- **Idea system performance is measured, reviewed, and improved.**

GUERRILLA TACTICS

Five actions you can take today (without the boss's permission)

1. Give extra attention to that first idea. When someone steps forward with his or her first idea, treat it with extra care. If the idea cannot be immediately implemented, explain why, or work with that person to overcome its limitations.

2. Make a personal commitment. What personal commitment can you make that will send a message to your employees that you will take their ideas seriously? Can you commit to a rapid response? Do not make a commitment that you cannot keep.

3. Help people with their ideas. When employees come to you with ideas that need some work to develop, help them to get the information or assistance they require. Build a network of people and resources in your organization that you and your employees can tap for help in this regard.

4. Pass it along. If a good idea pops up in your department that could also be used elsewhere, pass it along to the appropriate people. Conversely, look for good ideas elsewhere in your organization that you can bring back to your department.

5. Don't be stymied by bottlenecks in implementation. If your group is short of resources or skills to implement ideas in a particular area, look for creative solutions to the problem. Call in retirees on a temporary basis, recruit outside vendors, or offer your own people overtime. Do you have any assets you can redeploy or swap? Perhaps you can trade some of your people's time and skills to another department in return for the specialized skills you need.

CHAPTER 6

FOCUSING ON
WHAT MATTERS MOST

Once a good process to handle ideas has been set up, the next step is to think about how to focus employees on problems or opportunities of real importance. One might expect a narrower focus for ideas to lead to fewer of them. But the opposite is true. Alerting employees to problems or opportunities they may not have been paying attention to actually helps them come up with *more* ideas. When managers learn how to aim ideas at specific targets, they gain a powerful weapon.

When ideas are needed on a specific topic, the most straightforward thing to do is to *ask* for them. This conceptually simple tactic can be extremely powerful. The challenge is to identify the right issue, and to define it in a way that is meaningful to employees. The following example from one of LaSalle Bank's early idea campaigns illustrates this point well.

The first morning Juliette Sneed started working at the bank as an administrative assistant in the Automated Teller Machine (ATM) Services Department, five heavy boxes of documents were deposited next to her desk. They blocked part of the hallway and made it inconvenient for her to get in and out of her work area. The boxes sat untouched until the evening cleaning crew took them away for trash recycling. Sneed thought little of it. But the same thing happened the next day, and every day after that. None of the boxes were ever opened. Sneed asked a colleague about them and was told that the boxes contained printouts of the bank's daily ATM transactions nationwide. But no one needed them anymore, since the information was now available online.

Sneed called the printing department to tell it to stop producing the printouts, but it responded that it was only following procedures. She asked around about how to get the procedure changed, got nowhere, and eventually gave up. For *four years* the boxes were faithfully delivered every morning and taken away each night, unopened.

Then one day in 1999, she opened her paycheck envelope and found a note from Harry Tempest, the bank's chairman, announcing that the bank's new "IdeaCenter" was having its first idea campaign. The theme was "output management"—the elimination of unnecessary paper-based reports, memos and forms. A company-wide voicemail broadcast from Tempest followed soon afterward, reiterating how much the bank needed ideas in this area. She realized that the boxes of ATM printouts were exactly the kind of waste Tempest was talking about and immediately submitted a suggestion to stop producing them. The IdeaCenter responded quickly, thanking her for her idea, and within a matter of days the boxes stopped coming.

Consider what had been changed by Tempest's request. Before he articulated the need to reduce excess paperwork, ideas on this topic were not generally seen as important. They were not really *legitimate*. Front-line employees were not looking for opportunities to save paper, and even if they did notice some unnecessary paperwork, they would not have thought of sending in a suggestion to eliminate it. With his letter and voice mail, Tempest changed this.

But Tempest's request also legitimized such ideas for *managers*. It made them sensitive to paper-saving ideas as well. In effect, Tempest's call to action created a fast track for the type of ideas he was looking for—now the organization would welcome them and act quickly on them.

When ideas are needed on a specific topic, the most straightforward thing to do is to ask for them. This conceptually simple tactic can be extremely powerful. The challenge is to identify the right issue and to define it in a way that is meaningful to employees.

Legitimizing new categories of ideas can be a powerful way to enhance performance. Recall that in chapter 1, we described how John Hanson, Winnebago's founder, articulated the need for *weight-saving* ideas for one of the company's vehicle models. An entire topic of inquiry that had previously been overlooked by front-line employees immediately became the center of attention for them. Before, they had not considered weight to be a problem and so did not think about how to reduce it. Nor did their managers.

When Hanson asked for weight-saving suggestions, it gave his organization a small shock. Winnebago had always been careful about weight when designing its vehicles, but line employees had never been concerned about it. Tempest's initiative at LaSalle, on the other hand, was a major shock to his bank. It challenged the industry mind-set. The industry, both by habit and necessity, has always been highly conservative and proceduralized. Extensive documentation—which traditionally means paperwork—is the hallmark of the business. The last thing bankers would think of questioning was the need for record keeping, backup copies, and reports. It is safer to err on the side of having too much paper, rather than too little. This centuries-old and deeply ingrained bias was what Juliette Sneed initially encountered. But Tempest had now separated the issues of *documentation* and *paperwork*. Before, a manager might have legitimately worried about eliminating a report or dropping a name or two from a distribution list. Today, when an employee points out some unnecessary paperwork, the same manager might get in trouble for *not* taking action on it.

Although focused idea campaigns, like those of Winnebago or LaSalle Bank, have finite lives, their impact is enduring. Once a previously overlooked aspect of performance has been articulated and legitimized, and people have come up with large numbers of ideas for improvement in that area, the organization remains sensitive to it for quite some time. At LaSalle Bank, general awareness of the cost of unnecessary paperwork will encourage people to keep paperwork to a minimum as they develop procedures or design new products and services. Every time someone thinks about creating a new form or report, he or she is much more likely to question whether a paper version of it is really needed. In the long run, the most significant impact of the output management campaign will be a permanent shift in the way people think about the need for hard copy. In this way, a good idea campaign can subtly shift the operating assumptions of an entire organization.

It is worth noting that identifying critical areas for improvement and focusing people's attention on them can be done by any manager at any level and even by the employees themselves. We came across a good example of employees choosing focus areas at a Cummins Engine facility near Columbus, Indiana. The facility's primary improvement focus was on reducing the time taken to assemble the turbo-charged diesel engines that the company was building for the Dodge Ram series of trucks. While the overall goal was set at the top, the specifics were left up to the people actually assembling the engines. Each self-directed work team, consisting of six to eight people, was expected to identify and focus on the areas of greatest opportunity for reducing cycle time in its work cell.

Although focused idea campaigns have finite lives, their impact is enduring. Once a previously overlooked aspect of performance has been articulated and legitimized, and people have come up with large numbers of ideas for improvement in that area, the organization remains sensitive to it for quite some time. A good idea campaign can subtly shift the operating assumptions of an entire organization.

When managers let employees know what the critical issues are, make certain they understand why these issues are important, establish clear metrics, and invite their ideas, it increases alignment between the employees' concerns and the company's needs. But one should take note that this "Ask, and ideas shall be given you" approach works only when employees respect their managers. Once respect is established, employees are very willing to help out. Herb Kelleher, CEO of Southwest Airlines, found this out in early 2000, when his company was reeling from a huge increase in fuel prices. He sent a letter to the employees asking them for help. He wrote that if everyone could save just $5 per day, this would translate into company-wide savings of $140,000 a day. To emphasize his point, he ended his letter in this easygoing way: "Please accept this in place of your Year 2000 Valentine [an annual tradition at Southwest] which we are not sending because of high fuel prices. You are my Valentine." Within six weeks, employees had sent in ideas worth some $2 million. And that was simply because Kelleher and his management team had genuine credibility with employees, owing to their long history of listening to and acting on their concerns.

At roughly the time that Kelleher was asking employees at Southwest for ideas, a major steelmaker in the midwestern United States was trying to do the same thing. The company was in financial trouble because of its high production costs and fierce foreign competition. Management launched a company-wide initiative asking for cost-saving suggestions and offered substantial prizes, including new automobiles, for the best ideas. In the end, however, despite all its efforts and all the money dangled in front of workers, very few ideas came in. Management was surprised at the poor response, but the steelworkers we talked to were not. They had a uniformly low opinion of management—in fact, they were furious with it—because in their view, its long history of ignoring their suggestions for improvement was what had gotten the company into trouble in the first place. We were told story after story of almost scandalous neglect.

For example, one problem had plagued the continuous casting area for years. After the molten steel was poured into the caster, the solidifying white-hot steel slabs would emerge beneath it onto rollers that supported and guided them away as they cooled. Every so often, one of the rollers would lock up, either because it was jammed by debris or simply because a bushing seized up in the hot and dirty environment. The bad roller would drag on the soft slab of white-hot steel and gouge its surface. If not repaired, these defects would be magnified when the slab was rolled into thinner sheet steel, the form in which it was sold to customers. Before aggressive foreign competitors forced the steelmaker to pay more attention to quality, it was standard practice to ship this damaged product to customers anyway. But once customers had other options, they no longer had to put up with these blemishes, so that the company was forced to repair the damage before processing the slabs further. This repair work was both costly and disruptive, because the twenty-five-ton slabs had to be pulled off the conveyor lines and taken to a special area for refurbishing.

The frustrating thing for the workers in the casting area was that they spotted a defective roller almost immediately. Nevertheless, when they brought it to the attention of management, they would be told that instead of repairing it at once, it should wait until the next scheduled repair cycle, sometimes several days away. Meanwhile, the workers in this round-the-clock operation could only watch helplessly as the company lost money on every slab it produced. The recurring problem of the bad rollers—which they knew would be quickly fixed at many of their foreign competitors—was caused by exactly the kind of poor management that had caused repeated layoffs and pay cuts and that one day might well end up costing them their jobs.

A few years before the mill had launched its idea campaign, it had set up "Joint Improvement Teams," consisting of both managers and workers, to improve quality, productivity, maintenance, and safety. Although the meetings had generated many good ideas, managers rarely followed through on them. In time, they began skipping the meetings entirely. One worker told us that he and his colleagues believed the teams had been put in place only to placate major customers concerned about the company's quality improvement activities.

Given such a history, it is not surprising that so many employees viewed the idea campaign with disdain. What is more, one person told us, the steelworkers found the rewards insulting:

> *Although I've been working here almost thirty years, they [management] never gave me the chance to feel a part of the company. Now we are in trouble, and management thinks they have to bribe us to help. This is just one more way they remind me that I am not part of the team.*

Another worker, who operated diesel locomotives to transfer billets, molten pig iron, and finished steel, echoed his coworker's frustration and mistrust:

> *I have asked them at least ten times to fix the brakes on my engine before I kill someone. My pleas are consistently ignored. I have to work at half pace just to make sure I can stop in time. Why should I believe that they now want to listen to my ideas on how to make things better?*

Managers at this company had some work to do before they could get the ideas they wanted.

CHOOSING WHAT TO FOCUS ON

It is both a science and an art to select the right theme for employee ideas. In chapter 1, we discussed how the economist Friedrich Hayek classified knowledge into two types: knowledge of *particular circumstances of time and place* and *aggregate* knowledge. Generally speaking, front-line employees possess more of the first type of knowledge. But managers possess more aggregate knowledge—exactly the type of knowledge that is needed to identify where ideas will have the greatest impact on overall performance.

A lot of thought went into Tempest's selection of paperwork reduction as the theme for one of LaSalle Bank's early idea campaigns. The bank had made a series of acquisitions and was just completing a major strategic initiative to integrate purchasing across all of its North American operations. Using its size, the bank had negotiated good prices for office supplies but would save even more by consuming *less* of them. The idea of focusing on reducing paperwork arose in part because paper and printing costs were two of the items the company spent the most money on. As an internal study at the time put it:

A review of existing operating practices revealed that LaSalle Bank produces over 130 million pages of non-customer-related print output each year. This represents over 6,800 pages per employee and is exclusive of locally printed reports.

In addition to the direct savings from eliminating unnecessary paper and reports, every piece of paper that is produced creates ancillary costs. Someone must print and copy it, and forward it to the right people. The people who receive it have to review it, decide what to do with it, and possibly file it (requiring file folders, file cabinets, and space) or forward it to other people (requiring their time). Eventually, it must be archived (incurring further storage and handling costs) or purged from the files and thrown away (creating more costs in handling and disposal). One hundred thirty million pages of paperwork create a huge overhead. Another reason that Tempest selected paper reduction as a theme was the bank's strategic goal of moving toward more electronic storage and retrieval. But what was especially clever about focusing on paper was that it was a topic that every employee in the bank could relate to and do something about. In other words, the theme of his campaign was broad-based and strategic in nature, and it included *everyone*.

The LaSalle Bank campaign theme incorporated all the characteristics of an effective choice of focus for employee ideas. From management's perspective, paper reduction was a high-leverage way not only to reduce costs, but to meet several important strategic goals. The only way to root out excessive paper usage was to get everyone involved. Most of the opportunities to eliminate paperwork were relatively small and situation-specific, meaning *employees*, not managers, were in the best position to see them. It was a theme they could connect with—they were after all dealing with unnecessary paperwork every day—but most employees and managers had considered it a fact of life for anyone who worked in a bank. With good insight, both into what was important and what would resonate with employees, Tempest had turned the spotlight on a significant opportunity for improvement that the organization might otherwise not have been able to pursue.

Choosing a worthy theme for employee ideas begins with identifying the primary drivers of the department's, group's, or organization's performance. Generic high-level issues such as cost, quality, or customer service may be places to start but are usually too broad. To be effective, a theme should concentrate everyone's efforts on a specific actionable leverage point, perhaps a narrower dimension of the larger issue. Identifying leverage points usually requires thought, research, observation, and analysis. For an example of how this works, consider what happened at Coolman and Coolman, an Indiana home builder we worked with. Since this company depended heavily on advertising to sell its homes, managers began with the question "How do we make our advertising more effective?" After some investigation, however, the company found that people who responded to advertisements required a great deal more "selling" time and effort than those who were referred by previous customers, and they were much less likely to end up buying a new home. The question then became "How do we get more referrals?" The answer? Delight *existing* customers. But this was still too broad a concept. So more research was done.

The three most important factors to customers turned out to be quality, delivery, and the buying/building experience. "Quality" meant a home delivered as specified and defect-free. "Delivery" meant the house was completely finished by the promised completion date. And a good "buying/building experience" meant helpfulness at each stage of the process and supplying customers with full, timely, and accurate information. By focusing improvement ideas on these three items, referrals were increased more than *sevenfold* over three years, and advertising and selling costs were reduced. Before this idea initiative began, the company had delivered only *one home* in *twenty years* that was completely free of minor defects that had to be fixed after the customer moved in. After concentrating on such defects, Coolman and Coolman was able to deliver *70 percent* of its homes without any additional work needed—a standout performance in the residential construction industry in which "callbacks" are the norm. What began as an effort to figure out how to improve advertising had ended up, after investigation and analysis, identifying three points of high leverage for employee ideas.

Choosing a worthy theme for employee ideas begins with identifying the primary drivers of performance. An effective theme concentrates everyone's efforts on a specific actionable leverage point. Identifying such leverage points usually requires thought, research, observation, and analysis.

Focusing ideas can be done at any level of an organization. For example, the accounts receivable group in one division of a leading office furniture company we worked with was struggling with an average collection time of more than seventy-five days. Particularly puzzling was that most customers were large, credit-worthy companies. When managers in the department investigated the delinquent payments more closely, they discovered that most customers were perfectly willing to pay within the prescribed time but held up payment because of outstanding problems with the products. Such problems ranged from the wrong model of chairs being delivered to a mistake in the color of fabric. In hunting down the reasons for all these errors, the department found that over 90 percent of them could be traced to mistakes made when the original orders were entered. With all the options available for styles, dimensions, colors, and fabrics, it is understandable how sales staff, customers, and order entry personnel could easily make mistakes.

And so the accounts receivable department, together with the sales and order entry departments, asked employees for ideas on how to reduce errors in order entry. The results were impressive—collection time was reduced from seventy-five days to forty-five days, which injected tens of millions of dollars into the company's cash flow. And this was only the most directly measurable impact. Correct order entry cascaded into a host of additional savings systemwide and greatly increased customer satisfaction. It was by far the best and least costly place to catch mistakes. In other words, the group had chosen a point of high leverage for the entire company's performance as well.

Idea campaigns can be used to address a wide range of issues. We came across a unique theme at the Danish sugar company Danisco. When new European Union agricultural policies changed the competitive rules within its industry, this company was forced to close its sugar refinery on the island of Oland in the Baltic Sea. It asked its employees for ideas for new businesses they could start and that the company could invest in, so that they would have jobs when the refinery closed. In the end, the company got thirty-six ideas and gave the go-ahead to eight. Collectively, these created twenty jobs. And the fact that Danisco had already vetted the proposals and agreed to invest in the new businesses made it much easier for them to raise money from other sources, such as banks and local government. Moreover, the ideas came from employees, who, as longtime residents on the island, knew the area well. As a result, the start-ups fit local needs exceptionally well and turned out to be excellent investments for Danisco. When the company closed two other refineries a few years later, it ran similar campaigns.

MAKING FOCUS A WAY OF LIFE

Focusing ideas need not be a one-time or even an occasional activity. It can be incorporated more permanently and routinely into the way an organization operates. Recall from chapter 3 that Kacey Fine Furniture, the retailer in the Denver, Colorado, area, integrates ongoing targeted idea campaigns with its open-book management and quarterly performance bonuses. Once a year the management team identifies areas of focus where employee ideas will make a significant difference to the company's bottom line. Levels of performance improvement in these areas are tied to corresponding bonus pool amounts that everyone shares.

One year, for example, reducing customer returns was identified as a theme. Returned furniture is extremely costly for any furniture retailer. Not only is the customer unhappy and the sale possibly lost, but the company has to pay for the extra handling and transportation costs and often has to mark the furniture down in order to resell it. In the company-wide quarterly meeting that introduced the metric, Kacey's CFO explained to everyone that although the company's return rate was already better than the industry average of 10 percent of sales, if it could be lowered further, the impact on the bottom line would be significant. In this way, the return rate was put high on everyone's agenda, and with the idea system ready for employee ideas, the company got a lot of them.

One of the more novel suggestions was from an assistant truck driver. He had noticed a pattern in the way customers rejected furniture. Often, right after the piece had been delivered, they commented about how the same pieces that had looked so wonderful in the showroom seemed strangely out of place in their homes. Within a few minutes, he would watch them begin to think their purchase had been a mistake. Because Kacey's policy was to accept returns without question, he and his driver would then have to repackage the furniture and drive it back to the warehouse.

The assistant truck driver realized that the reason the furniture looked more attractive in the showroom was that it was arranged by professionals. His idea was to give the company's nineteen truck drivers and their assistants some of the same training in interior decorating that was given to the salespeople. If the truck drivers and assistants understood more about the subject, he reasoned, they could help customers integrate the new pieces of furniture better into their homes. The idea was given the go-ahead, and the truck drivers and their assistants were given the training.

A primary part of the training was about how to properly "accessorize" a new piece of furniture—that is, arrange other items around it, such as lamps, potted plants, side tables, and pictures—to personalize it and create the desired effect. Now, when delivering a sofa, for example, the delivery crew does not simply ask, "Where do you want it, lady?" Instead, before bringing it in, they find out why the customer bought the new furniture, visit the room it will go in, and look for appropriate accessories.

Together with the customer, they develop a plan. When the crew retrieves the sofa from the truck, they are able to position it nicely and accessorize it stylishly. With their decorating help and willingness to please, these truck drivers greatly improve the chances that customers will like their new furniture and generate considerable word-of-mouth advertising. Their new professionalism has given Kacey considerable competitive advantage. The other furniture companies in the area contract out the delivery process. *Their* delivery people still knock on the door and ask, "Lady, where do you want it?" It is worth noting that the idea of giving drivers training in interior decorating could *only* have been successful if it had come from a driver. Imagine the response from the drivers if the idea had come from management.

Focusing ideas need not be a one-time or even an occasional activity. It can be incorporated more permanently and routinely into the way an organization operates.

A well-thought-out policy can be just as effective as a bonus program in inspiring ideas on specific topics. When Grapevine Canyon Ranch launched its idea system, some of the early ideas dealt with inequities in tipping. The wranglers got a preponderance of the tips because they had the most personal contact with customers. The rest of the employees, who were working just as hard for the guests behind the scenes, received relatively few. After the problem was brought up in several idea meetings, it was decided to change the tipping policy. From then on, guests were asked to tip only when checking out and were told that their tips would be shared equally among the employees. The wranglers' resistance to this change quickly subsided when they discovered themselves earning *more* in tips than they did before. Because guests were now tipping as a percentage of their total bill, there was a lot more money in the pool. Customers also liked the new policy. They no longer had to worry about when it was appropriate to tip or about carrying cash while engaged in activities around the ranch.

While the Grapevine policy change did resolve concerns about tipping inequity, it also focused employee ideas on high-leverage opportunities for improvement. *Every* employee now had a vested interest in making each guest's stay as enjoyable as possible. The ideas that came up in the weekly meetings quickly reflected this. Many were simple comfort suggestions such as "Make sure there is a cooler with cold drinks in the van that goes across the desert to pick up and deliver guests to the Tucson airport," or "Improve 'way-finding' signs so guests can find their cabins more easily—especially in the dark." As so often happens, many ideas both improved the customer experience and made people's jobs easier. For example, one of the cooks suggested that breakfast be served buffet style, rather than à la carte, so guests could have faster service, and those who were running late for a morning activity could still get something to eat. Not only was the new buffet very popular with guests, but fewer waiters were needed in the dining room, and the stress of running a short-order breakfast service was eliminated.

Another idea was to start the morning rides earlier during the summer, so the guests could enjoy the desert before it got too hot. This suggestion posed a challenge. The wranglers who were out with the previous evening's ride would have to get up extra early to prepare the horses—a process that took several hours. A series of employee ideas cut this time by more than 60 percent. Even the horses benefited. They no longer had to stand around for long periods of time before and after being saddled, and they were back in the barn before the temperature became unbearable.

Another example of a company that has used policies to focus ideas is Wainwright. The company had articulated a hierarchy of values—in descending order, these were *safety, people, quality, customers,* and *profit*—and the reasoning for it was this: Safety was primary because it affected the company's people. People delivered high quality. High quality satisfied customers, and customers generated profits. Everything stems from safety. This company value was reinforced constantly through the company's weekly and monthly idea lottery drawings, in which every employee got lottery tickets for each idea he or she submitted. Safety-related ideas, however, had a separate drawing for prizes, which dramatically increased the odds of winning. This was a clever way to highlight the importance Wainwright placed on worker safety and to keep people sensitive to it. At the time we last visited the company, there had not been a lost-time accident in over three years, and the company had workers' compensation costs significantly lower than its competitors.

KEY POINTS

- If management needs ideas on a specific topic, the most straightforward thing to do is to ask for them. This conceptually simple tactic can be very powerful.

- A good theme for employee ideas is simple to understand and measure, takes advantage of critical interrelationships that drive bottom-line results, and resonates with employees.

- Focusing ideas need not be a one-time, or even an occasional, activity. It can be incorporated permanently into the way an organization operates. Bonus programs or well-designed policies can be effective tools in this regard.

GUERRILLA TACTICS

Five actions you can take today (without the boss's permission)

1. Select your targets. Look for areas where employee ideas can help improve performance. To do this, think about the following:

- The major problems or opportunities facing your group

- The aspects of performance that have the greatest impact on the organization's overall performance

- The non-value-adding things that your group does

- Which key corporate goals and values, when translated into your area, might yield appropriate targets for ideas

Once you have come up with an appropriate topic, ask your people for ideas related to it.

2. Focus on your customers. Which aspects of your group's work are most important to your internal and external customers? What are they complaining about? What changes would they like you to make? Would they appreciate faster response time? Have your people talk to customers directly. Discuss what they find out, and develop appropriate themes for ideas from it.

(continued)

3. Poll your people. Ask your employees where *they* think improvements are most needed. Get them involved in identifying appropriate areas to target that they can attack with their ideas.

4. Use metrics. Identify your group's key performance metrics, post performance statistics on them for everyone to see, and keep them up-to-date. Set targets, and review them regularly at group meetings.

5. Look for ideas that reinforce core values. What are the values you want to instill in your group? Teamwork? Responsiveness? Seamless integration? Exceptional service? Uncompromising quality? Find creative ways to focus ideas on topics that reinforce these values.

CHAPTER 7

GETTING MORE
AND BETTER IDEAS

In chapter 1, we described what happened when one of the world's largest airlines subjected all its employees to creativity training and ended up frustrating them and making management look stupid. The multimillion-dollar initiative naturally led employees to believe that the company was eagerly awaiting their ideas. But when they returned to work, they found it just as unresponsive as it had always been. The real bottleneck to ideas all along had not been the *employees'* lack of creativity but *management's* inability to listen to them. A great number of organizations have made a similar mistake. It makes little sense to waste resources stimulating more ideas from employees, if you can't handle the ones they *already have.*

Once a healthy idea system is in place, however, it makes a lot of sense to help employees come up with more and better ideas. This chapter is about how to do so.

———■————————

HOW PEOPLE COME UP WITH IDEAS

The starting point for thinking about how to help employees come up with more and better ideas is to understand how people spot problems and opportunities, and develop ideas from them. Consider the following example.

Less than a year after copilot Chris Moran began flying for American Airlines, business slowed, and he was furloughed along with six hundred other pilots. Because of his experience in the U.S. Air Force, he was able to get hired as a scheduler at American's Miami hub. His job was to coordinate passenger demand, crew schedules, gate availability, equipment options, maintenance requirements, and the capability of different airports to handle various types of aircraft. He was also expected to take cargo into account, but like the other schedulers, he paid little attention to it.

During a slack period, however, he began wondering about cargo and decided to look into this side of the business. During his seven years in the air force, he had flown a lot of freight. He called some of the managers in the cargo division and asked to meet with them. They were a little surprised. Schedulers *never* visited cargo. Their decisions had always been based on passenger loads. At best, cargo was an afterthought.

At that initial meeting, the managers told Moran that cargo was immensely profitable for the airline, with margins approaching 40 percent. The problem was that the routes with high *passenger* loads often did not match the routes with high *cargo* demand. An example of this was the Dallas–Omaha route, where the passenger traffic was low but the demand for mail cargo was high owing to Omaha's huge insurance industry. Nevertheless, the route was assigned Fokker 100s, relatively small commuter jets that were able to carry little more than passengers and luggage. The same problem occurred on Latin American routes, where the passenger traffic was highly seasonal, but demand to transport fruit and flowers north to the United States and Canada was consistently strong. Even so, as passenger demand dropped, the airline would take an airplane like the Boeing 767-300 off these routes and replace it with the 767-200, which had considerably less cargo capacity. This meant that the cargo sales team could not make commitments to potentially large customers who wanted to contract for steady shipping capacity. As a result, American Airlines often lost valuable cargo business. Even when passenger considerations were *completely* taken care of, cargo was still ignored. Airplanes like the MD-80 and the Boeing 727 were scheduled interchangeably because they had similar seating capacities. But the 727 could carry a lot more cargo. With minimal coordination and investment, Moran realized, the airline could dramatically increase its cargo revenue.

Once a healthy idea system is in place, it makes a lot of sense to help employees come up with more and better ideas. The starting point for thinking about how to do this is to understand how people spot problems and opportunities and develop ideas from them.

Moran spoke with his boss, who encouraged him to explore the idea further. Soon, Moran discovered another problem. Each airport provided a list of the types of aircraft it could handle. He found that, at many airports, either the information on the list was incorrect, or an unlisted aircraft could easily be accommodated. For example, several airports listed as lacking the appropriate equipment to handle certain types of aircraft had actually acquired the equipment but had neglected to report it. In other cases, the only reason certain aircraft were barred from particular airports was that the stations hadn't gotten around to painting stopping marks next to the jetway for those particular aircraft. Correcting oversights like these vastly increased scheduling flexibility.

In the end, Moran was able to demonstrate that in the top twenty-five cargo markets, American could make more money flying *freight* than passengers. He sent in an idea: Create a position on the scheduling staff for someone with a cargo background, who could incorporate freight considerations into aircraft scheduling. The idea was accepted for a one-year trial, during which cargo revenue jumped by $7 million. Today, cargo information is formally incorporated into the computer models American uses for scheduling.

The question we want to ask here is this: Why was it Moran who spotted this opportunity? American Airlines had been shipping cargo since its inception. For decades, hundreds of routing experts and operations researchers had been optimizing everything from fares and routing to fuel consumption and equipment purchases. Yet they had missed a huge opportunity that was right under their noses. But Moran had not. Why?

The reason is that his background in cargo gave him a different *perspective* from the other schedulers, one that led him to ask questions they did not. But his perspective alone didn't give him the idea he came up with or the justification for it. For this, he also needed *knowledge* of the situation, which he obtained through his research. This is how ideas arise—a person with the right perspective and knowledge is in the right place at the right time.

The late policy analyst Aaron Wildavsky made an interesting observation: *A difficulty is only a problem if something can be done about it.* Problems and opportunities remain invisible to people who are unaware of better alternatives, or at least the possibility that these might exist. To increase the number of problems and opportunities their people spot, managers have to provide them with appropriate training and experiences. We classify these employee development approaches into two general categories. First is direct training in *idea activators*—to give employees profound knowledge in areas where their ideas can have the biggest impact. Second is exposure to new situations and experiences that will broaden their perspectives.

IDEA ACTIVATORS

One of the pioneers of the modern idea system was Toyota. In the early 1950s, the company initiated a long-term drive for performance improvement, with the goal of just-in-time production. As inventory was reduced and processes were linked more tightly, smaller and smaller problems seriously disrupted production. The company was forced to pay extraordinary attention to detail, and managers alone simply couldn't spot every tiny problem. The company had to ask its front-line employees for help and eventually developed a very active idea system.

Over time, Toyota introduced training programs to help employees come up with many more ideas. Instead of showing people how to do specific tasks, these programs showed them how to improve key drivers of performance, such as quality, productivity, and safety. We have come to call such training programs *idea activators*, because their purpose is to spark more and better ideas by giving people a deeper understanding of their work. Some of Toyota's activators are as follows:

- **"Poka-yoke," or error-proofing.** A *poka-yoke* is a simple way to ensure that a certain kind of mistake—one that people are prone to making repeatedly—can no longer happen. It is an empowering and easy-to-learn method that helps people come up with a great many ideas.

- **"5S," or rigorous housekeeping.** A good 5S training program sensitizes people to all kinds of ways they can become more productive. The five *S*'s are *seiri* (putting things in order), *seiton* (arranging things efficiently), *seiso* (preventing problems by keeping things clean), *seiketsu* (doing after-work maintenance and cleanup), and *shitsuke* (showing discipline, following the rules). Anytime it takes people more than a few seconds to find something, they will ask themselves why. Simple concepts—such as air-free and shallow storage schemes, and the importance of using vertical space—make it possible to store things more conveniently, using less space. A decade after Toyota Kentucky began 5S training, managers there told us that employees were still coming up with thousands of useful 5S ideas each year.

- **Quick changeover (QCO).** The principles behind quick changeover can be taught in several hours and result in employees thinking of all kinds of ideas that they might not otherwise. With enough ideas, the length of time it takes to change machines over from making one part to making another can be reduced from hours to minutes.

- **Total productive maintenance (TPM).** TPM involves a brutal measurement, "overall operational effectiveness," to highlight problems that most organizations miss. With the advent of TPM, managers accustomed to reporting flattering efficiency levels—above 90 percent, say—find themselves sheepishly reporting overall operational effectiveness levels of maybe *30* to *40* percent. Opportunities for improvement that they had not seen before become quite obvious.

Toyota's idea activators are well suited to the way it manufactures automobiles. But every organization has different needs and has to develop idea activators appropriate for its own situation. To clarify what we mean, let us look at an example from the health care industry.

The late policy analyst Aaron Wildavsky observed that *a difficulty is only a problem if something can be* *done about it. In other words, problems and opportunities remain invisible to people who are unaware of better alternatives, or at least the possibility that these might exist.*

Good Shepherd Services is a not-for-profit health care organization with a ninety-six-bed nursing home, located in northern Wisconsin. Its mission is to provide its residents with the best quality of life possible. To do this and to be financially viable in an industry that is under tremendous pressure to keep costs down, it strives to use best practices throughout its operations. This means that front-line employees—the certified nurse's aides (CNAs) and other staff who have primary responsibility for the day-to-day care of the residents—have to know these best practices well, apply them, and develop new ones. While the typical health care organization is extremely hierarchical, with direct care staff having little input into how things are done, Good Shepherd gives them a great deal of autonomy to develop strategies and ideas to personalize the care of each of their charges. To help them do this, the organization uses six idea activator modules, each two to three days long:

- Observing and Understanding the Older Adult

- Elimination and Incontinence (on the causes of incontinence and how to address them)

- Skin Care (on the causes of skin breakdown and the treatment and prevention of pressure ulcers)

- Psychosocial Well-Being (on how to address difficult resident behaviors, and how to reduce or eliminate the need for restraints)

- Falls and Restorative Care (on preventing and reducing the severity of falls, and holistic restorative care for optimal functionality)

- Nutrition (how nutrition can affect the outcomes of specific kinds of interventions)

Each of these modules is designed to make caregivers aware of the latest thinking and best practices in the area. The sessions are developed by national experts using the latest research and are delivered by highly skilled practitioners. They provide new knowledge and understanding from which front-line employees can develop ideas to help their residents and better individualize their care. The following examples illustrate how this works.

The first module we described briefly in chapter 1. The most common reason why older people enter nursing homes is dementia—severe loss of memory and cognitive capability, to the point where it is difficult for them to function normally. With these residents, safety is a primary concern. Among other things, they must be kept from wandering into potentially dangerous places—such as kitchens, offices, and boiler rooms—by special bracelets, which trigger an alarm when they enter these areas. On one particular door, the alarm used to go off constantly. Whenever it did, staff members had to immediately break off whatever they were doing and run to find the now-distraught resident and escort him or her back to safety. In one of the Psychosocial Well-Being training modules, the staff learned that people with dementia often avoid dark spots on the floor, because they see them as holes. One aide had the idea of painting the floor black in front of the troublesome doorways. When her team implemented the idea, it eliminated the problem.

Idea activators are training modules that give employees profound knowledge in areas where their ideas can most help.

The second most common reason why people are admitted to nursing homes is incontinence, an embarrassing problem for anyone. To sensitize staff to the difficulties their charges face, before attending the incontinence training module, each person is required to interview some incontinent residents. The interview consists of two questions: "What is it like to be incontinent?" and "If you weren't incontinent, how would your life be different?" A great many staff members have been shocked to learn how drastically the condition changed their residents' lives.

The Incontinence module explains the four main causes of incontinent episodes. One of them, for example, is that an elderly person becomes disoriented, perhaps when waking up at night, and loses track of where the bathroom is. This piece of information led to many ideas to help residents know where the bathroom is at all times. For example, when building or remodeling bedrooms, always position the toilet so that it is easily visible from the head of the bed. Similarly, when considering the way furniture is laid out, think about line of sight to the toilet.

Since the Incontinence training module began, Good Shepherd has been able to reduce the percentage of its residents who are incontinent to levels well below national and state averages despite the fact that it takes a much higher-than-average percentage of incontinent residents. As a result, Good Shepherd now does *one ton* less laundry per month and spends *six thousand* fewer hours (more than 3 full-time equivalents) per year dealing with incontinent episodes.

At most nursing homes, the biggest cause of injuries is falls. Among other things, the module on falls teaches the importance of tracking data. One staffer noticed that a disproportionate number of falls were occurring several hours before breakfast. Her group studied the phenomenon and discovered an important fact. Because Good Shepherd is in rural Wisconsin and many of its residents used to live on farms, they were accustomed to getting up early. They continued to do so at Good

Shepherd, where they were often walking around well before breakfast. Naturally their blood sugar levels decreased, so they felt faint and weak and were more likely to trip or fall. The staffer's idea: Put out trays of muffins, toast, juice and coffee a few hours before breakfast. The problem was solved. Using ideas like these, Good Shepherd has been able to reduce the number of falls from an average of some forty per month to about ten.

Many of the ideas triggered by the idea activators are specific to individual residents. For example, one dementia resident was pinching the caregivers every time they lifted him in or out of his wheelchair. He would grab hold of the fleshy underpart of their upper arms so hard that he would give them bruises and cause them real pain. The standard solution would have been to put him on powerful psychoactive drugs.

But the Psychosocial Well-Being module had taught that there were many different ways to handle behavioral problems other than heavy medication. The staff asked for two weeks to come up with a better solution. They contacted the resident's former social worker and learned that before the resident had come to Good Shepherd, his family had dealt with him by duct-taping him into his bed. The man wasn't trying to *hurt* the nurses; he was merely clinging to them in fear. The care team came up with the idea of buying thick cooking mitts for him. From then on, when the staff needed to move him, they put the mitts on him, and he was able to hang on without hurting anyone.

Good Shepherd's idea activators have done their job—they have increased the ability of line staff to come up with ideas, ideas that have significantly improved the quality of their residents' lives.

HOW TO BROADEN EMPLOYEES' PERSPECTIVES

Idea activators boost the quantity and quality of ideas in specific and predetermined areas. More broadly based approaches to helping people come up with ideas involve giving them greater perspective on the organization and their work. Following are examples of some of these.

Job Rotation

Koji Kobayashi, former chairman of NEC, believed that "Job rotation is the miracle drug of productivity." Job rotation gives employees different perspectives on how the company operates. It allows them to make connections they otherwise might not make, as Chris Moran did with his cargo idea at American Airlines. Furthermore, when people understand more about how the company operates, their ideas will be better and have greater impact, and they themselves will become more effective idea champions.

An MBA student from Thailand pointed out to us that rotating *managers* can also help employees come up with more ideas. Her father owned a number of hotels and resorts, and he rotated his senior management team every two years. The rotations were deliberately radical; that is, the head of accounting might become the head of housekeeping, while the head of customer service might be put in charge of food services. After each rotation, the number of ideas submitted would invariably soar. The reason was this: When an executive took over a totally unfamiliar department, he or she was unusually open to ideas about how to improve it, and the employees knew this.

Adopting the Customer's Perspective

Customer complaints are excellent sources of ideas because they identify problems. Consequently, organizations should make it *easy* for customers to complain and encourage employees to use complaints as starting points for improvement ideas.

But complaints alone represent only part of the customer perspective and happen only *after* a problem occurs. Being proactive in getting to know customers and their needs—through surveys, focus groups, shadowing techniques, mystery shoppers, "psychographics," or simply by talking with them—can provide a wealth of ideas. In his book *Winning at New Products*, Robert Cooper (creator of the Stagegate process) identifies lack of market orientation—that is, not putting the voice of the customer into the development process from beginning to end—as one of the most common reasons why new products fail. Plenty of excellent books, articles, and training seminars are available on techniques for getting customer input. The trick is to get this input to the employees who can use it. Good Shepherd, for example, has quarterly "Care-Planning" meetings with every resident and his or her family. Any complaints or special requests become fodder for ideas.

This does not mean customer ideas should be followed *literally*. Although customers may be aware of problems, they are not necessarily in the best positions to figure out how to solve them. In the 1990s, the Scandinavian airline SAS extended its internal idea system to its customers. It was an interesting idea that backfired. SAS found itself having to spend considerable time explaining to customers why their ideas could *not* be implemented, for reasons that were relatively obvious from the airline's point of view. Customers knew little about the systems and processes that they were proposing quite specific changes to.

Many employees don't deal with external customers directly. But everyone has *internal* customers—people who depend on what they do. Sensitizing employees to the perspectives of these customers and to the importance of asking their input, can also stimulate a great many useful ideas. We came across one of our favorite examples of this in a Baldrige examiner training session a number of years ago.

Idea activators boost the quantity and quality of ideas in specific areas. More broadly based approaches involve giving people greater perspective on the organization and their work. These include job rotation, adopting the customer's perspective, ongoing learning, benchmarking, reading groups, and more.

A hospital gave its staff members internal customer training as part of a quality initiative. For one of her class assignments, a nurse interviewed an intake clerk from radiology to see whether that department was getting all the information it needed from the completed form her group sent down with each referred patient. When she asked how the information on the form was used, she got a surprising response. Radiology, it turned out, used only *two* of the twelve items on it. For years, the nurse realized, her group had been asking unnecessary questions of thousands of patients, diligently logging the answers, and sending them to a department that did not want them.

Cycle-time Reduction

There is a lot of truth to the tired old cliché "Time is money." Generally speaking, the faster an organization gets things done, the more productive it is.

Looking at work from the perspective of reducing the time it takes is an excellent way to spot new problems and opportunities. Time is easily measured and people readily see when they are wasting it. A good number of the ideas discussed in this book began when someone decided it took too long to do something. Teaching people the importance of reducing cycle time, and the general principles of how to do it, can trigger a large number of good ideas.

Ongoing Learning and Development

Almost by definition, learning broadens people's perspectives. Not all learning is directly relevant to the workplace, but organizations can promote the kinds that are in all sorts of ways. The most obvious is to support employees who wish to take classes, finish their formal education, or work toward another degree or advanced certification of some kind.

Less formal learning opportunities—such as trade shows, professional meetings, and study trips—are valuable, too. With a sense of purpose, these trips can be *better* sources of good ideas than traditional classroom-based learning. In the classroom, students are taught what the instructor thinks they ought to know. With more informal learning, people seek out what is most interesting or important to them—information or know-how that connects with a need they recognize.

Offering these informal educational opportunities to frontline employees can pay huge dividends. Danisco, the Danish sugar company, regularly sends its front-line employees to trade shows or on study trips to other companies, and they often come back with good ideas. For example, a maintenance worker went to a conference in Göteborg, Sweden, where he happened to attend a presentation by a welding company. He learned about a new type of hardened metal, and it gave him an idea.

Danisco makes sugar from beets. When the beets are brought to the mill, they are dumped into a hopper outside, mixed with water, and then pumped inside for processing. During the harvest season, the huge pump involved moves some six thousand tons of beets every twenty-four hours. Because the beets came directly from the fields, they were covered with stone and dirt, and the slurry was extremely abrasive. The tips of the blades inside the pump used to wear down quickly. Every year, a maintenance team would have to take the pump apart to replace them. When the maintenance worker learned about the new hardened metal at the conference, he realized that blades tipped with this metal would last much longer. His idea was implemented, and now the pump has to be disassembled only once every *seven* years.

Another effective form of ongoing learning is reading. It is common for managers to buy books they like and distribute them to their employees. But without follow-through, nothing much usually happens. Not everyone reads the book, and those who do, do so in isolation. A good way to add the necessary follow-through is to set up a reading group.

Reading groups are flexible and can be designed for a wide variety of purposes. They may be limited to a single concept or book, or they can be part of an ongoing development program. We have learned several important lessons about how to run effective reading groups. First, the group should be large enough to ensure diverse perspectives but small enough so that everyone can be actively involved. Depending on the mix of personalities in it, a good size is six to ten people. Second, meetings should be regular and properly spaced so as to maintain continuity yet allow participants time to do their assignments justice. Usually, a period of two to three weeks between meetings works well.

Finally, having a skilled outside facilitator adds credibility to the process, if he or she has expertise beyond what is in the books and practical experience applying the concepts in them. He or she can create a nonthreatening environment that gets everyone involved and can make it safer to challenge the organization's existing orthodoxies.

Reading groups can result in profound changes in perspective. In 2001, we conducted one for the management team of a unit of one of the largest telecommunications firms in the United States. The first book assigned was *Built to Last,* by Jim Collins and Jerry Porras. It is about what differentiates organizations that thrive over a period of decades, from those that don't. In the very first meeting, the top manager opened by saying, "I felt *heartsick,* just *heartsick,* reading this book. I realized that this organization wasn't built to last. We are essentially a bunch of start-ups that were bought and merged, and we have never done any of the things we need to do to be viable in the long term." Think of how a change in perspective like *that* could open the unit to fresh ideas!

Benchmarking

Benchmarking involves looking outside the organization in an effort to stimulate performance improvement ideas. When employees see other organizations doing things significantly better, their eyes open to the fact that there is room for improvement in their own operations. Benchmarking is not about copying—it is meant to be a spur for ideas. That is why Granite Rock, the construction supply company and 1992 Small Business Baldrige Award winner, benchmarked its delivery processes against Domino's Pizza.

Another company that benchmarks extensively is Sewell Motors, a network of highly successful car dealerships in Texas. Owner Carl Sewell, author of the best-selling book *Customers for Life,* has benchmarked against companies as diverse as Chuck E. Cheese, MacDonald's, and Disneyworld.

The approaches we discussed in this section were designed to help people see their organizations from different perspectives and to incite them to come up with more and better ideas. But sometimes having the appropriate perspective and relevant knowledge isn't enough. Something more is needed.

IMPROVING ALERTNESS TO PROBLEMS AND OPPORTUNITIES

In 2001, Thomas Cantelmo, an American Airlines flight attendant, suggested a change in the procedure for handling coffee pots on airplanes. Before his idea, the pots were replaced with fresh ones after every flight, even on trips less than an hour long and even if the pots had not been used. He proposed loading coffee pots on only the *first* flight of each day and washing them out and reusing them throughout the day. After all, on longer flights the pots were already being washed out and reused a number of times. His idea was implemented, and the savings were calculated at $788,000 per year.

Why was Cantelmo the one to think of this idea? Plenty of other people had the same opportunity. The catering process had been designed by professionals—*they* might have thought of it. The purchasing department, which had negotiated in detail the contracts for airport services might have thought of it, let alone the *tens of thousands* of other flight attendants on literally *millions* of flights who had used the same pots for several decades. Furthermore, most, if not all the employees who could have spotted this opportunity were on the lookout for *exactly* this kind of cost-savings idea. Robert Crandall, CEO from 1983 to 1998, had been relentless in his drive to cut costs. The idea system that he had started was a giant cost-cutting engine that every employee was aware of. With a 10 percent reward for money-saving ideas, anyone in the airline who noticed a way to save $788,000 in costs would have immediately sent in an idea. But Cantelmo didn't think of the idea because his perspective was different from those around him or because he knew more than they did. He was simply more *alert* than they were.

Once people have perspective or knowledge that sensitizes them to the importance of ideas in a particular area, their ability to come up with ideas depends on how alert they are. The question then becomes how to increase one's level of alertness. Cantelmo told us that his training at the U.S. Naval Academy had taught him to pay attention to detail and always to look for the meaning behind what he observed.

One person who thought a lot about how to sharpen his senses was Leonardo da Vinci. In the book *How to Think Like Leonardo da Vinci,* author Michael Gelb tells of how many of da Vinci's startlingly original ideas came from his uncanny ability to notice things. It was a gift that da Vinci worked hard to develop. For example, to strengthen and test his olfactory powers, he would collect a variety of flowers, pile them on a table, blindfold himself, and try to recognize them by scent as his servant held each to his nose. Whether or not these exercises actually helped, his senses were certainly acute. He was able to draw pictures of the wing motions of birds in flight that no one could corroborate for hundreds of years until the advent of high-speed photography proved him right.

---

*Once people have perspective or knowledge that sensitizes them to the importance of ideas in a particular area, their ability to come up with ideas depends on how alert they are. Prolific suggesters **discipline** themselves to notice "exceptions," **record** their thoughts and observations, and are willing to **spend time** studying the problems or opportunities they spot.*

Da Vinci also did more conventional things to improve his powers of observation—things we have come across others doing as well. Whenever we meet employees who are unusually prolific suggesters, we like to ask them how they come up with so many ideas. Frequently, they tell us about homegrown methods to do two things that da Vinci regarded as of primary importance. First, they *discipline* themselves to notice "exceptions"— things that seem odd or out of place. Second, they *record* their thoughts and observations.

Many ideas begin when someone notices an exception of some kind. A good example of this was the employee at Johnson Controls who saved her company $80,000 a year when she noticed some items sticking out of the trash that shouldn't have been there. She realized that employees on the assembly line were putting parts in their pockets for convenience as they worked and were throwing them away when they discovered them as they left work. Her idea was to place special recovery bins by the exits to the facility, with signs reminding people to check their pockets on their way out. In the early 1990s, we asked the top suggester at Honda's flagship plant near Tokyo how she had been able to give in more than *two thousand* ideas in the previous year. Her reply? "I don't overlook exceptions."

The second thing prolific suggesters often mention is that they *write their thoughts and observations down*. In a typical example, at Marabou, a division of Kraft foods in Sweden, we talked with an employee who had consistently come up with several hundred ideas every year. When asked how he did it, he smiled and pulled a small dog-eared notebook from his back pocket. He carried it everywhere, he said, and whenever he noticed something that wasn't quite right, he wrote it down. From time to time, he would look over the list. Whenever an idea occurred to him that had to do with one of the problems on the list, he would get out his notebook and write the idea next to that problem.

Many researchers who have studied the creative process have noticed how highly creative people usually keep some kind of notebook, diary, or journal. After outlining the various things that Leonardo da Vinci did to keep himself alert, one of the first pieces of direct advice Gelb offered his readers was this:

> Keep a journal or "notebook." Leonardo da Vinci carried a notebook with him at all times so that he could jot down ideas, impressions, and observations as they occurred. . . . For da Vinci, the process of recording questions, observations, and ideas was of great importance.[1]

By the end of his life, Leonardo had accumulated seven thousand pages of notes.

A third characteristic we have noticed in prolific suggesters is the willingness to *spend time* studying the problems or opportunities they spot. Chris Moran's research into cargo operations uncovered all kinds of information that was important in formulating and championing his idea. Likewise, it took the staffer at Deutsche Post (discussed in chapter 1) months of legwork and experimentation to discover how his company could buy cheaper engine oil for its diesel trucks. Many ideas require considerable research before they can be realized.

IDEO, the California product design company made famous by the *Nightline* segment "Deep Dive," uses a creative problem-solving process with several nice touches. The most important of these, in our opinion, is that the fact-finding stage emphasizes *deep research* into the problem at hand. Teams are sent out to study intensively all aspects of the product, what it is intended for, and how it will be used. The extraordinary depth and scope of this research allow IDEO to notice things that a less rigorous research phase would undoubtedly miss and so to come up with superior designs that have some impressively novel and practical features.

Another way to improve one's alertness is to learn to be sensitive to change. Remember how change creates the need for further change? Since everything changes constantly, fresh problems and opportunities arise all the time. However, sometimes people have been working under one set of assumptions for so long that the problems and opportunities created by a new situation are invisible to them.

Consider what happened at Cloetta, the largest candy manufacturer in Sweden. One of its product lines is hard candy, which is made from a stiff sugary "dough" extruded into its final shape by machines. Before the dough is put into one of these machines, it has to be kneaded and worked. For decades at Cloetta, this kneading had been done by hand, on four special tables. Since the dough hardened quickly at room temperature, the surfaces of the tables were heated by hot water pipes running underneath. And because the heated tables were used around the clock, they were left on all the time.

In 1981, the company purchased a new extruding machine that was able to knead the dough as well. Two of the four heated tables were no longer needed. People soon began using them as convenient places to set down tools, gloves, and ingredients. Since the company still had one of the older machines that required dough to be hand kneaded, the other two heated tables continued in operation until 1996, when this last machine was replaced. These tables, too, were soon littered with miscellaneous work items.

In 1997, a year after this latest change, one of the workers in the room sent in a suggestion. Since the tables were no longer used to knead candy, he pointed out, why not shut off the heaters underneath them? For *sixteen years*, without anyone noticing, the company had been keeping two of the unused tables heated around the clock, and the other two had been unnecessarily heated for the last year! Not only did this cost money, but since a *lot* of heat was involved, it had made the room so unbearably hot that the company had to invest considerable money in cooling it down.

In this particular case, the same people who no longer had to do the kneading on the heated tables continued to suffer from the heat, simply because they had become accustomed to it. The force of habit obscured the possibility of turning it off. What is more, during all this time, Cloetta employees were *on the lookout* for ideas. The company had one of the best idea systems in Sweden. It was a classic case of what some management theorists refer to as the "Boiled Frog Syndrome."

Supposedly, a frog dropped into a pot of boiling water will jump out immediately. But if it is put in a pot of cool water, which is then slowly brought to the boil, the frog will stay put until it boils to death. The conclusion drawn from this dubious assertion[2] is that sudden and dramatic negative change is obvious to people, but if the same change creeps in gradually, people can remain oblivious to it for a long time. And if people find it hard to detect fresh problems (i.e., negative consequences of change) when they are introduced gradually, how much harder is it for them to detect *opportunities* (i.e., the potential for positive change when things are already working satisfactorily) that may arise in the same unobtrusive way?

The need for a further change in a chain of changes can also be missed for another reason—namely, the division of labor. Change occurring in location A creates the opportunity or need for further change in location B, but different people work in locations A and B, and the people in B aren't aware of the change in A. It is surprising that this kind of communication breakdown can still occur when A and B are physically very close to each other.

Take, for example, what happened in the forestry division of a state government in New England. In early 2001, a forester working in a state park came across a locked telephone box deep in the woods. Wondering what it was for, he made some inquiries when he got back to the office. It didn't take long for the accountant in his office to track down what it was. In the mid-1980s, that same office had installed seventeen phones in remote areas of the forests to allow the foresters to check in when they were out in the field. The problem was that in the mid-1990s, the extension service had issued cell phones to all its foresters. But no one had thought to cut off the old land lines, and the division had been paying the monthly charges for them ever since.

When the forestry service bought cell phones, someone should have asked what the cell phones would allow the service to do differently. But there was no single person who was in a position to see the whole picture. Even though the same department paid both bills, it is easy to imagine how no one there would question them. For all the administrative assistant knew, the phone boxes might have had other uses as well. Even the foresters who were issued with cell phones and knew about the phone boxes might have assumed the same thing. Or maybe they assumed that the phones had been disconnected and would be removed later. Anyway, now that they had cell phones, foresters didn't have to follow the same paths through the forest as they had done before, and so might well have forgotten about the phone boxes. There are all kinds of ways that the organization could have overlooked the presence of the unneeded phone boxes.

The important thing is to realize that *every* change—whether initiated inside the organization or outside—can create either the opportunity or the need for a further change. When change occurs, it is a good time to be alert for another possible change. Ask the question "What new opportunities does this change create?" And after addressing these, ask the question again.

KEY POINTS

- Once an organization has an idea system in place, it should take action to help employees come up with more and better ideas.

- Every idea results from a mix of a person's *knowledge* related to the problem or opportunity and the *perspective* he or she brings to it.

- The late policy analyst Aaron Wildavsky observed that *a difficulty is only a problem if something can be done about it.* Problems and opportunities remain unnoticed by people who are unaware of a better alternative, or at least the possibility that one might exist. This is the rationale behind the two main ways to increase the quantity and quality of employee ideas: increase people's knowledge and expand their perspectives.

- Idea activators give employees a deeper understanding of critical areas where their ideas are particularly needed.

- Managers can help their employees gain different perspectives on their work in many ways: job rotation, benchmarking, listening to customers, ongoing learning, reading groups, study missions, and trips to conferences and trade shows.

- Once people have perspectives that sensitize them to the importance of ideas in a particular area, their ability to spot a specific problem or opportunity often comes down to their alertness. Unusually prolific suggesters discipline themselves to *notice* exceptions, *record* what they observe, and spend time *studying* the problem or opportunity.

- Change creates the need for further change. Unfortunately, the force of habit often blinds people to the need for these subsequent changes. Whenever change occurs, it is important to ask, "What new opportunities does this change create?"

GUERRILLA TACTICS

Five actions you can take today (without the boss's permission)

1. Train, train, train. Identify the key leverage points of performance for your group, and develop idea activator modules for them. They don't have to be long; sometimes fifteen minutes is all that is needed. Stay alert for possible activators as you read business books and magazines, interact with colleagues, and look over mailers from training companies.

2. Get out of the office. Attend trade shows, workshops, and conferences. Take advantage of opportunities to visit other companies, including ones that do very different types of work. Bring some of your people along whenever possible.

3. Record exceptions. Ask your people to record any exceptions they see. From time to time, probe these exceptions with your group to see whether they suggest any improvement opportunities.

4. Rotate your people. Rotate your employees into different assignments, so they see as much of the organization as possible. Approach your internal customers and suppliers, and ask whether they would be interested in trading people for short periods of time. The resulting alliances, and the exposure your people get to new perspectives and knowledge, will lead to more and better ideas.

(continued)

5. Encourage diverse perspectives. Ask people who you think might have a different perspective on your department's work for their thoughts on how it might be improved. New hires, temporary workers, people who work odd shifts, recent transfers, and internal customers are all potential sources of fresh perspectives.

CHAPTER 8

LIBERATION AND TRANSFORMATION

In 1892, National Cash Register had a large shipment of defective cash registers returned from Great Britain. When the company's CEO, John Patterson, investigated the source of the defects, he was shocked to discover that the registers had been sabotaged by his own employees. He realized that their morale was extremely low, because of how poorly they were treated. He immediately set about turning the situation around. Among other things, he started up a suggestion box system, the first in the United States. Because of his prominence in the business world at the time and the forcefulness with which he advocated the benefits of employee ideas, the suggestion box became a popular management tool in the first half of the twentieth century.

Like Patterson, many early business leaders saw the suggestion box as a tool to counteract a problem that concerned them deeply. As their organizations grew in size, they became increasingly impersonal, and employees found it harder to feel ownership in their work. Forward-thinking managers saw the problems this disengagement created. The prevailing view at the time was that the benefit of a suggestion box lay not in the ideas themselves, but in reengaging employees with their work. When the National Association of Suggestion Systems was founded in 1942, its primary goal was "to improve employer–employee relations."[1] Only later would it change its name to the Employee Involvement Association.

Today, a great many organizations still struggle with poor cultures. Although most managers would agree that a dysfunctional culture results in lower performance, elements of culture such as trust, respect, commitment, and involvement are difficult things to manage. Because of this, many managers who have attempted to improve their organizations' cultures have met with disappointing or ambiguous results.

But organizations with effective idea systems have learned that there is a strong link between culture and the flow of employee ideas. This is why an idea system—whose performance can be *measured* and *managed*—provides such an effective way to improve corporate culture. In this chapter, we tell the stories of organizations that discovered the connection between culture and ideas, and used this discovery to break into much higher levels of performance.

IDEAS AND ATTITUDES

In chapter 2, we described how the idea system at Grapevine Canyon Ranch created a considerable competitive advantage for it. But this was not the reason that CEO Eve Searle started her idea initiative in 1993. At the time, she was merely looking for a way to change her employees' negative attitudes toward their work.

One day, an ad for a seminar put on by Boardroom Inc. caught her eye. The seminar was about the company's idea system, and among other things the ad claimed that listening to ideas from employees would change the way they felt toward the company. Intrigued, Searle decided to attend. She came away with the message that a good idea system might indeed improve her employees' attitudes. This rang particularly true to her. As a young woman, Searle had worked in a number of companies where she had proposed better ways to do things, only to have her bosses rebuff her. And she had always remembered how that felt.

Although most managers would agree that a dysfunctional culture results in lower performance, elements of culture such as trust, respect, commitment, and involvement are difficult things to manage.

When she got back, she started regular idea meetings with a small group of employees whom she thought would like to offer ideas. The group met every two weeks, and each person was asked to bring two ideas to every meeting. Sometimes Searle asked for ideas on a particular theme, such as how to cut costs, how to improve efficiency, or how to enhance guest services. As ideas began to get implemented, other employees asked to participate in the meetings too. Over time, Searle was able to make the meetings a company-wide activity. By 1996, idea meetings were a fixture at Grapevine Canyon. Every two weeks on payday, she ended up with ten to fifteen good ideas.

Searle never imagined the depth and extent of the change her idea system would bring about. She hoped for *some* improvement in morale but not the "total turnaround" (as she put it) that ultimately transpired. Her customer satisfaction ratings soared. Not only did employees become genuinely concerned about looking after the guests, but their ideas included a myriad of nice touches that made life easier and smoother for everyone—including themselves. What was totally unexpected, however, was the effect of her new idea system on the *horses*.

In 1992, a number of the ranch's horses had suffered bouts of colic (irritated bowels). The national average for a stable of horses is roughly one case of colic per year for every hundred horses. When, within a two-month period, two of her seventy horses died of colic, and seven others came down with it, Searle knew she had a problem. Colic causes discomfort to humans, but for horses (who have some three hundred feet of intestines) it can be life-threatening. Colic can be caused by a food obstruction, worms, or general poor health. In an otherwise healthy horse, it can be caused by stress.

To Searle's surprise, from 1993 (when Grapevine started its idea system) to 1998, there were *no further* cases of colic at the ranch, a rate far below the national average. During a short period in 1998, after a new wrangler with some personal problems was hired, there were four cases of colic. But once that wrangler left, there were no further cases. What Searle discovered was that horses are extremely sensitive to negative attitudes in their handlers. In fact, they react *physically*. When Searle started her idea process, she certainly did not expect the resulting cultural transformation to lower her veterinarian bills substantially.

As Searle put it, a good idea program turns "them" and "us" into "we." The increased interest of her employees in their work, together with their improvement ideas, translated into a more productive and enjoyable work environment for everyone—guests, employees, managers, and even the horses.

—■——————

IDEAS AND RESPECT, TRUST, AND INVOLVEMENT

In 1991, Ray Winter took over as president and chief operating officer of BIC Corporation. During his introductory meeting with the employees, it became obvious to him that he had a problem. As he put it, "It's very difficult to speak to 650 people knowing that they don't believe a word you say, and who think that *your* job is to eliminate *their* jobs." BIC had recently opened several new plants in the Carolinas to produce roller pens. The workers at the Milford, Connecticut, facility (company headquarters and the base of most of its production) were convinced the move was the first step in transferring production to right-to-work states to break the union. Rumors were also in the air that the company was considering relocating much of its manufacturing to Mexico. Employee–management relations could hardly have been worse. Several employees told us that during those times they would not have risked speaking to their supervisors without a union steward present. Winter saw immediately that the poor employee–management relations were the predominant reason for the organization's high costs and were what was keeping it from improving. He promptly made it his highest priority to turn the situation around.

One of his initiatives was to encourage each of the eight largely autonomous profit centers in the company to develop a strategy to increase employee involvement. But after a year or so, it became clear that things hadn't changed much. The reason was that the term *employee involvement* had never been clearly defined. As Winter put it, when two people passed each other in the hallway and waved, this was deemed to show employee involvement. This vagueness left the company with no real way to track and improve how it was doing in regard to the president's top priority. Essentially, his managers were navigating blind.

But the Ink Systems Unit was a different story. When asked to work on employee involvement, its director Dick Williams had asked a group of union workers to help develop their unit's approach. One of the things this group pointed out was that they and their colleagues had a lot of ideas on how to make the operation run better but kept these ideas to themselves, because they didn't believe the company would listen to them. With Williams's encouragement, the group set up a process for soliciting and handling ideas, and they asked Charlie Tichy, a union worker and outspoken critic of many management practices, to run it. It was an enlightened choice. If a hardened union workforce was going to be convinced that the company was ready to take their ideas seriously, who better to convince them than one of their own?

In short order, the program became very successful. The 130 hourly employees in the Ink Systems Unit submitted some 300 ideas in the first three months, and some 1,200 ideas in the first year, an average of more than nine per person.

The Ink Systems Unit's success with its idea system showed Winter the connection between the *number of ideas* his employees were offering and the *level of their involvement*. If the employees submitted lots of ideas, they were clearly involved. Conversely, if they were involved, they would submit ideas. In short, employee ideas provided a way to manage involvement. Finally, BIC had something it could measure and improve. Why not, Winter asked, simply define the "employee involvement" program to *be* the idea system?

---

*Organizations with effective idea systems have learned that there is a strong link between culture and the flow of employee ideas. This is why an idea system—whose performance can be **measured** and **managed**—provides such an effective way to improve corporate culture.*

From that moment, things gelled quickly. Dick Williams was promoted to vice president of manufacturing, and the idea system was implemented company-wide as a joint labor–management initiative. Tichy served as one of the two co-coordinators of the program, and Philip Preston, a veteran union worker recently promoted to management, as the other. In 2002, the company received some three ideas per employee. The performance improvement and cost savings from the system have been significant, and labor–management relations are greatly improved. The idea system served its purpose of getting employees more involved and increasing their trust in managers. By doing so, it removed a barrier to progress.

Winter observed that the idea initiative also taught his *managers* respect for their employees. Managers learned that their employees could make them look very good, if only they let them.

—■———————

IDEAS AND INTERPERSONAL RELATIONS

Remember DUBAL, the highly successful aluminum company in Dubai? When its CEO John Boardman said, "Our idea system *is* our competitive advantage," he was referring to much more than the ideas directly related to business operations.

Dubai is a very international community. Some 80 percent of DUBAL's 2,700 employees come from abroad. In 2002, its workforce was composed of nationals of forty-three countries. At DUBAL this diverse labor force has learned to work together— and work together *well.*

The idea system proved an invaluable instrument for creating harmony and making the company more welcoming to people with substantial differences in their cultural and religious backgrounds. Because most of its employees live in company housing, DUBAL encourages ideas that address lifestyle needs. For example, Sikh employees suggested that a place be provided for them to worship, observing that the company already had a church, a mosque, and a Hindu temple. So a small Sikh temple was built. When Filipino workers pointed out that the cable channels the company provided didn't include one of the most popular ones in their country, that channel was added. And many suggestions have come in—and been responded to—about what kinds of foods to provide and how to prepare them.

In similar companies around the Persian Gulf, the typical foreign worker might stay with a company for three to five years.

DUBAL has an incredible *3 percent* turnover rate, and many of its expatriate employees have been with the company for more than twenty years.

All kinds of synergies accrue to DUBAL because of the "harmony" resulting from its smooth-running idea system. Because its workforce is stable, the resources invested in training have more impact. DUBAL has a substantial training budget, averaging several thousand dollars per employee per year. Without the need to train many new employees, this budget goes mostly into deepening the skills of the existing workforce. Because of this, over time the skill level of the workforce has increased dramatically.

HOW IDEAS COUNTER LEARNED HELPLESSNESS

Ed Schultz, former CEO of Dana Commercial Credit (now part of Dana's leasing operation), always paid keen attention to the culture in his organization. He told us that he had been sensitized to the importance of culture as a small child:

> *My father used to come home at night from the wire mill, and he would be laughing, and I would ask him why. He would tell me about something stupid management was doing down at the plant. And I would say, "Why don't you tell them?" He would say, "First of all, they are not interested in my ideas, and second, they don't care."*

This comment reveals how helpless Schultz's father felt because his ideas weren't listened to. He dealt with this by poking fun at management and emotionally distancing himself from the company. His was a case of what psychologists call "learned helplessness." When people are constantly beaten down and reminded on a daily basis that they aren't supposed to think, sooner or later they stop showing any initiative. Conversely, when employees' ideas are encouraged and used, their energy, commitment, and initiative increase. Consider the following example.

Mark, a student in one of our classes, worked weekend nights at a five-star hotel in Chicago. His job was to close accounts and prepare guest bills for the following day. The overnight crew was largely leaderless—if problems developed, the employees on duty were expected to solve them themselves. One Saturday night, about 10:30, the entire Detroit Lions football team arrived for a game the next day with the Chicago Bears. The team was ravenous, and as soon as they checked into their rooms, they all ordered room service. The night shift in the kitchen was completely overwhelmed.

One guest, who was not a member of the football team and who was staying in one of the $700-per-night luxury suites, called the front desk to complain that he had ordered room service ninety minutes earlier and still didn't have his food. Mark went down to the kitchen, found the guest's order in the chaos, expedited it, and personally took it up to the luxury suite. When the guest answered the door, Mark wheeled the service table in and turned to face the disgruntled guest. Addressing him by name, he explained what had happened and said, "This type of service is totally unsatisfactory for our hotel. We cannot in good conscience charge you for your stay tonight." He gave the guest this complementary stay on his own authority.

In the morning, Mark's supervisor came in. As usual, Mark reported on the night's activities, including how he had waived all charges for the guest in the luxury suite. Rather than being upset, his manager complimented Mark for his actions and suggested that Mark lead a team to identify how similar problems could be avoided in the future. What is more, the next day, the customer called, complimented the manager on Mark's quick action, and reserved the luxury suite for a ten-day stay the following month.

When people are constantly beaten down and reminded on a daily basis that they aren't supposed to think, sooner or later they stop showing any initiative. Conversely, when employees' ideas are encouraged and used, their energy, commitment, and initiative increase.

It is worth noting that Mark could just as easily have chosen to duck the problem with the guest in the luxury suite and passed him on to room service. His boss could not have criticized Mark for not exercising initiative, nor would the frustrated guest have really blamed him in any way. After all, it was management that failed to foresee the room service bottleneck.

Managers cannot foretell the future. Employee initiative is often critical. In the normal course of things, by the time Mark's manager would have learned of the service failure, it would have been too late. But Mark's quick action made the hotel and his manager look good. And when Mark's courage and initiative were appreciated, he became a more confident person, and so a more valuable employee.

For a manager, the difference between looking stupid or looking brilliant can be as simple as being open to a subordinate's perspectives and ideas. In other words, a good idea system is a potent antidote to the kind of culture that Scott Adams pokes fun at in his Dilbert cartoons. As Schultz put it, when talking about his father's experience:

> *I never really understood why it was that no one would listen to a person who has spent twenty-five years running the same piece of equipment and knew everything there was to know about that piece of equipment. When you stop and think about it, it is categorically ridiculous for them not to. They are missing so much that their employees go home at night laughing at them.*

IDEAS AND A HIGH-PERFORMANCE CULTURE

Throughout this book, we have tried to show how employee ideas help managers improve both performance and the cultures of their organizations. In this final section, we recount the journeys of two organizations: Milliken & Company and Good Shepherd Services—one a major global corporation, and the other a modest not-for-profit health care organization. Both are in intensely competitive industries. In the beginning, both had leaders who faced difficult situations and took bold steps to change the way their organizations worked. And in both cases, employee ideas were key to the transformations that put them solidly out in front of their competitors.

The story of Milliken's idea initiative began in 1980, as the company was moving into a wrenching downturn. The textile industry has always been cyclical, and Milliken, like its competitors, was accustomed to ups and downs. Business in 1978 and 1979 had been good, but toward the end of 1979, orders began to drop off. Management knew a downturn was coming but was concerned that this one might be devastating. Dramatically increased foreign competition promised to force more severe price cutting than usual and make orders more difficult to attract. By the end of 1979, it was clear that the industry was in a full recession.

Every year, Roger Milliken, the sixty-five-year-old company patriarch, spent two weeks at the end of the year with his family in Vail, Colorado. While he did do a little skiing, he spent most of his time reading the latest business books. The management team had grown accustomed to Milliken coming back full of enthusiasm about some new management idea he had read about on his holiday. The year 1980 was no different. This time, he was excited about Philip Crosby's new book *Quality Is Free.*

Milliken was impressed by Crosby's assertion that even if a company was well managed, 22 to 28 percent of what it did was waste. In the *very* best ones, the figure was between 18 and 22 percent. "Even if our waste is currently only 10 percent," Milliken told his managers, "reducing it further is the best opportunity we have to work on."

Crosby's approach was a completely different way to manage quality than the one that Milliken & Company had been using. "It involves teams and all kinds of things to help people identify problems," Milliken explained to his management team. "It sounds exactly like what we've been hearing that the Japanese are doing to attack our automobile industry. Don't you think we ought to do this?"

Tom Malone, a vice president on the senior management team, wondered whether the others were thinking what he was: "Mr. Milliken has read another book. What changes will this one lead to?" He was certainly not prepared for what Roger Milliken proposed next.

"I tell you what. Let's get Crosby up here *today*. It says in the book that he lives in Winter Park, Florida. John [Rampey, vice president of education], call him up, tell him we are going to send a plane down to bring him up this afternoon, and talk about this." No one dared to remind Milliken that it was Sunday.

Half an hour later, Rampey came back.

"What did he say?" Milliken asked.

"He doesn't work on Sundays." The management team exchanged glances. *Wow*. Who *was* this guy, to talk to Roger Milliken like that?

"Well, go back and tell him we'll send a plane down in the morning for him."

A little while later, Rampey came back. "He won't come. He's not free. But if we send a plane down tomorrow, his company's president will come and give us an hour's presentation."

And that is what happened. After the presentation, Roger Milliken was even more enthusiastic. But Crosby was so swamped that it would be another two months before he could visit the company to give a seminar for its top one hundred managers.

Crosby's seminar was stimulating and inspirational, but his most significant contribution came during a private talk with Milliken. "If you implement this program," he said, "it will represent a radical change in the way you manage and lead people. And *you* can't lead it by yourself, because you have been managing the company in the same way for forty years.

"The only way you can change your culture," Crosby continued, "is to find a *horse* in your organization and challenge him to pull the company forward by leading the transformation in his area. *Your* job is to put scorecards in place. Create one for everyone on your management team, make sure you review them every four weeks in your policy committee meetings, and let your horse do his work. Let everyone see the results. You are going to have to manage the process, because otherwise your managers will gang up on your horse and kill him, and kill you with him. And then nothing will change in your company."

Employee ideas are key to building a culture of high performance.

Sometime later, Roger Milliken asked Malone to take a walk on the headquarters grounds. Milliken told him of his conversation with Crosby and then said, "Maybe you will be my horse." Nothing more was said on the topic by either man for the rest of the walk.

But Malone was shaken and more than a little concerned. What exactly did Milliken expect of him? The other members of the policy committee had been with the company at least fifteen years longer than he. He was the new kid on the block. Now he was being set up to lead radical change and be an example for the whole company! That night, he told us, he did a lot of thinking.

In the morning, Malone called Milliken and asked him whether he was serious about turning around the way the company was managed and about him leading the initiative. Milliken told him he was. Malone made two requests.

First, he asked for a free hand. He would, of course, keep Milliken informed, but he needed the authority to make major changes on his own. Second, he asked Milliken not to come to any of his divisional meetings for a year or to send any of his staff. (Milliken had an eighteen-person support staff who re-ported directly to him and were known throughout the company as his eyes and ears.) "The reason is that we are talking about a fundamental change in the way we lead our company. If you, or any of your people, are in the room, everyone will be watching you or them, not me. I will be simply a young kid who may not have a job in a year. With every decision, my people will be look-ing to see whether you or your staffer have your heads down or your eyes lowered. This would undermine our efforts to create real change."

Milliken thought for a moment. "What about a year from now?"

Malone replied, "I hope by then that our changes will have brought such good results that the entire company will want to come and see what we have done."

Over the next year, Malone's division underwent a dramatic transformation in the way it was managed. To showcase the new empowered work environment, Malone initiated quarterly "sharing rallies," in which small teams could present the im-provements they had made in areas such as quality, cost, deliv-ery, and safety. He also established an idea system, known as the OFI (Opportunity for Improvement) system. The OFI concept originated from one of Crosby's fourteen steps—Error Cause Re-moval (ECR). For a while, Malone's division had struggled with how to implement the ECR philosophy. The OFI system came from a plant manager in the automotive division, Wayne Punch. He had become interested in how to involve associates (Mil-liken's term for employees) in the ECR process and decided to implement an idea process in his facility. To make it clear that he was serious, he put in place a "24/72" policy—every idea would be acknowledged within twenty-four hours and re-sponded to within seventy-two hours.

As Punch explained it to us, the ideas came "pouring in," and his management team quickly realized that the process wasn't organized well enough to follow through with them as fast as his policy promised. So he and his management team asked the associates for help with implementation and advice on how to improve the process. Gradually the OFI system emerged. Once the process was working well, as Punch put it, "The motivation and morale of my people was just phenomenal. I became very excited to go into work because I had people who were smiling and excited about what they were doing."

Punch's plant produced such outstanding results that Malone adopted the OFI concept for his entire division and integrated it into the sharing rallies. Punch was later invited to teach the OFI process in the company's Pursuit of Excellence training classes, taken by managers from throughout the company. When Roger Milliken attended one of these classes, he liked what he saw, and soon the OFI process was adopted company-wide. As Punch commented to us, "I think of the OFI system as a recipe for becoming world-class in *anything*."

In the end, Roger Milliken and Tom Malone successfully led the company on the journey of total cultural change that Crosby had envisioned. Today, Milliken & Company has one of the best idea systems in the world. It is also one of only two companies ever to have won *both* the United States' Malcolm Baldrige National Quality Award and the European Quality Award.

A similar transformation took place at Good Shepherd Services. When Mary Ann Kehoe took over as managing director in 1991, the nursing home was in bad shape. Morale was extremely low, employee turnover was over 100 percent per year, and the organization was in financial trouble. In the eleven years since fourteen churches in the Seymour, Wisconsin, area had founded the not-for-profit organization, it had had *ten* different managing directors. When Kehoe took over, everyone wondered how long *she* would last.

Long-term care is a tough industry with a bad reputation. Because patients are often helpless, they can be easily exploited. Consequently, nursing homes operate under intense scrutiny by federal and state regulatory agencies and are subject to strict rules. In addition, the government Medicare payments that nursing homes depend on have not kept pace with rising costs, so money is often tight. Pay is low, especially for front-line workers, and turnover is high. Many nursing homes are forced to operate understaffed or to rely on temporary workers. For the people providing the direct care, the work can be quite unpleasant—much of their time is spent cleaning up after episodes of incontinence and dealing with patients with dementia.

Good Shepherd had been established to provide high-quality long-term care for the local community. Kehoe realized that unless Good Shepherd changed the way it operated it certainly could not fulfill this mission and might not even survive. She thought the answer lay in greater efficiency.

One of the industry's most serious problems is the wasteful way it delivers care. As an experienced nurse, she had seen much of this waste herself and knew that improved work practices would make people's jobs easier, save money, and enhance patient care. She also knew that many of the ideas on how to improve care would have to come from front-line staff, because they were the ones dealing with the residents. The problem was that the rules-driven hierarchical culture common in the long-term care field gave those on the front lines little chance to be heard. Kehoe also realized that simply asking front-line staff for their ideas wasn't going to be enough. If Good Shepherd was to apply *best practices* throughout its operations, direct-care staff needed more knowledge about the state of the art in long-term care. Then they could apply this knowledge, through the ideas they came up with, to improve the day-to-day care of individual residents. This was the genesis of Good Shepherd's idea activators discussed in the last chapter.

As the care staff gained experience working with ideas, they began to identify impediments to efficient decision making and implementation. They approached management with suggestions on how to improve the situation. Over several years, the leadership team made a number of crucial modifications to the way the organization worked. One, for example, ended the traditional practice of continually rotating staff between the facility's four wings (a wing has about twenty-four residents) and the different shifts. A series of suggestions had made it clear that this practice detracted from the staff's ability to come up with, agree on, and implement improvements. Not only did they work with different people every day, but they were not with individual residents long enough to get to know them well.

Knowing how to promote employee ideas will become a critical core competency for managers—and will become one soon. Mastery of this competency will separate effective managers from ineffective ones.

So Good Shepherd created permanent care teams, one for each shift in each wing. The teams consisted of nurses, certified nurse's aides (CNAs), dietary aides, and housekeeping staff. The stable team membership allowed employees to get to know the residents better, learn their individual needs and personalities, focus ideas on improving each one's quality of life, and work to-gether to develop and implement these ideas. Of all the idea systems we have come across, the one at Good Shepherd is the most integrated into the daily routine—so integrated, in fact, that it has almost disappeared. In other words, ideas are not merely central to the job at Good Shepherd, they are an indistinguishable part of the work.

This modest, community-based nursing home has come to have one of the best performance records in the United States. Although Good Shepherd takes residents who are in significantly worse shape than the nursing home average (as measured by state and federal acuity levels), it consistently outperforms industry averages on *every* major quality-of-life indicator, including incontinence, mobility, pressure ulcers, and social well-being. At Good Shepherd we found a warm, friendly, and welcoming environment. Members of the staff were professional and attentive, and they always had time for the residents. The residents were active and engaged and seemed to enjoy being there. Quite simply, we have never seen a better nursing home.

At the time of this writing, Good Shepherd had not been cited for a single deficiency by state or federal inspectors in over *eight years*. As far as we know, this perfect record is unmatched in the industry. The average nursing home gets eight deficiency citations *per year*. Employee retention at Good Shepherd is better than 90 percent, and there is a waiting list of people who want to work there. Employees who do leave—for higher wages or more convenient working hours—often return because they prefer the work environment at Good Shepherd.

Perhaps the best way to sum up where employee ideas have taken Good Shepherd is through a comment made by William L. Minnix, president and CEO of the American Association of Homes and Services for the Aging (AAHSA), the primary advocacy group for long-term care. As he said to Tommy Thompson, U.S. secretary of health and human services: "Mr. Secretary, I have seen the answer to our problems with good long-term care. It is in Seymour, Wisconsin."

---■---------

PARTING THOUGHTS

The Good Shepherd and Milliken stories illustrate why we use the term *revolution* to communicate what we saw happening wherever managers were seriously seeking and acting on employee ideas. Not only were they achieving results they had not thought possible, but they were doing it with fewer resources. They were running fundamentally different organizations.

And that is why we believe that future generations will look back on the way we treat our people and be puzzled by the enormous human potential we waste, and how much that waste is costing us. Organizations like Milliken and Good Shepherd are the ones that will survive and prosper in an increasingly competitive world. Those that ignore their most valuable resource will not. Like the CEO of the AAHSA, we believe we have seen the future of management.

Our parting thought to the reader is this: Knowing how to promote employee ideas will become a critical core competency for managers—and will become so soon. Mastery of this competency will separate effective managers from ineffective ones. If, after reading this book, you share our belief, *embrace* the subject. Do the same thing you do to sharpen your other professional skills. Keep up-to-date with the latest thinking and practice. Read, attend conferences and seminars, and network with like-minded people inside and outside your organization.

Visit organizations that successfully promote ideas (you may find them in some surprising places). But, most important, start asking your people for ideas. Remember, ideas are free, and they have the power to liberate your people and transform your organization.

KEY POINTS

- Most organizations struggle with dysfunctional cultures, and most managers would agree that a dysfunctional culture results in lower performance. The problem is that elements of culture such as trust, respect, commitment, and involvement are difficult things to measure and manage.

- Many of the best idea systems began with the aim of improving some aspect of the corporate culture.

- Organizations with good idea systems have learned that there is a strong link between culture and the flow of employee ideas. This is why an idea system, whose performance can be measured and managed, provides such an effective way to improve corporate culture.

- Knowing how to promote employee ideas will become a critical core competency for managers. Mastery of this competency will separate effective managers from ineffective ones.

- Join the Idea Revolution. Ask your people for their ideas.

NOTES

Chapter 1

1. Friedrich Hayek, "The Use of Knowledge in Society," *American Economic Review* 35, no. 4 (September 1945): 519–30.
2. "Modernizing Government," British government white paper, March 1999, 62.
3. For more on the I-Power system, see Martin Edelston and Marion Buhagiar's book, *I-Power: The Very Simple Secret of Business Success* (Greenwich, CT: Greenwich Institute for American Education, 1992).

Chapter 2

1. George Stalk and Thomas Hout, *Competing against Time* (New York: Free Press, 1990), 76.
2. Stalk and Hout, *Competing against Time*, 77.
3. James Abegglen and George Stalk, *Kaisha: The Japanese Corporation* (New York: Basic Books, 1985).
4. The *National Annual Report on Japanese Kaizen Teian Systems* (Tokyo: Japan Human Relations Association, November 1997), and the 1985 *Annual Statistical Report* of the National Association of Suggestion Systems (Chicago: National Association of Suggestion Systems, 1985). The U.S.

data are reported for the 1985 calendar year, the Japanese data for the 1986 fiscal year (April 1, 1985, to March 31, 1986). Savings for both countries are given in U.S. dollars at the exchange rate of $1 = 130 yen.

5. Peter Senge, *The Fifth Discipline* (New York: Currency Doubleday, 1990).

6. Chris Argyris and Donald A. Schön, *Organizational Learning* (New York: Addison-Wesley, 1978).

7. This point has made by a number of people. See, for example, Robert W. Weisberg, *Creativity: Beyond the Myth of Genius* (New York: Freeman, 1993).

8. Allan Nevins papers. Quoted from Ron Chernow, *Titan: The Life of John D. Rockefeller, Sr.* (New York: Random House, 1998), 180.

9. Julian Richer, *The Richer Way* (London: Emap Business Communications, 1995).

Chapter 3

1. Alfie Kohn, *Punished by Rewards: The Trouble with Gold Stars, Incentive Plans, A's, Praise, and Other Bribes* (New York: Houghton Mifflin, 1993), 17.

2. Steven Kerr, "On the Folly of Rewarding A, While Hoping for B," *Academy of Management Executive* 9, no. 1 (1995): 7.

3. Sources: The *National Annual Report on Japanese Kaizen Teian Systems* (in Japanese) (Tokyo: Japan Human Relations Association, November 1992), and the 1989 *Annual Statistical Report* of the National Association of Suggestion Systems (Chicago: National Association of Suggestion Systems, 1989). The U.S. data are reported for the 1989 calendar year, the Japanese data for the 1989 fiscal year (April 1, 1988, to March 31, 1989). Savings for both countries are given in U.S. dollars at the exchange rate of $1 = 130 yen.

4. This story is based on interviews with James Lisec (Krishan Jagga died in the early 1990s), on documents he sent us, on two articles about this court case in the *Wall Street Journal* (the front-page article in the February 23, 1976 issue and the short article about the wrongful discharge lawsuit in the November 8, 1985 issue, p. 10), and on the California Appeals Court decision *James K. Lisec et al. v. United Airlines Inc.* (1978) 85 Cal. App. 3d 969, and California Appeals Court decision *James K. Lisec et al. v. United Airlines Inc.* (1992) 10 Cal. App. 4th 1500, p. 2.

5. California Appeals Court decision *James K. Lisec et al. v. United Airlines Inc.* (1992) 10 Cal. App. 4th 1500, p. 2.

Chapter 4

1. Frederick Taylor, *The Principles of Scientific Management* (New York: Harper 1911; reprinted by Hive Publishing Company, Easton, Pennsylvania, 1985, p. 38.
2. Frederick Taylor, "Boxley Talk," June 4, 1907, Taylor Collection, Samuel C. Williams Library, Stevens Institute of Technology, Hoboken, NJ, p. 3. We are grateful to Robert Kanigel for alerting us to this quote in his book *The One Best Way* (New York: Viking, 1997), 169.
3. Martin Edelston and Marion Buhagiar, *I-Power: The Secrets of Great Business in Bad Times* (Greenwich, CT: Boardroom Books, 1992).
4. W. G. Dauphinais and C. Price, eds., *Straight from the CEO* (New York: Simon & Schuster, 1998), 243.
5. The source for the information in this paragraph is *Toyota: A History of the First Fifty Years* (Toyota City, Japan: Toyota Motor Corporation, 1988).

Chapter 5

1. G. W. Dauphinais and C. Price, eds., *Straight from the CEO* (New York: Simon & Schuster, 1998).

Chapter 7

1. Michael Gelb, *How to Think Like Leonardo da Vinci* (New York: Delacorte, 1998), 57.
2. In a somewhat distasteful experiment, a consulting company actually tried this with live frogs, and it didn't work as advertised.

Chapter 8

1. Lucas Frederick Sterne, "A Historical and Critical Analysis of Employee Suggestion Systems in American Industry," Ph.D. dissertation, University of Iowa, 1944, 29.

INDEX

ABOUT THE AUTHORS

Alan G. Robinson is an award-winning author, an educator, and a consultant. He is co-author of *Corporate Creativity,* which was a finalist for the Financial Times/Booz Allen & Hamilton Global Best Business Book Award, and was named "Book of the Year" by the Academy of Human Resource Management. He has a Ph.D. from the Johns Hopkins University and a B.A./M.A. from the University of Cambridge. He teaches at the Isenberg School of Management at the University of Massachusetts at Amherst. Dr. Robinson has advised more than a hundred companies and government agencies in eleven countries.

Dean M. Schroeder is the Herbert and Agnes Schulz Professor of Management at Valparaiso University. Prior to entering academe, he founded and led two companies, and as an outside CEO, led the turnaround of a third. He is the author of more than sixty articles and papers, several of which have received national awards. He served for five years on the Board of Examiners of the Malcolm Baldrige National Quality Award and is on the Board of Directors of the American Creativity Association. He has a Ph.D. in Strategic Management and a B.S. in Engineering from the University of Minnesota, and an M.B.A. from the University of Montana. Dr. Schroeder has advised companies all over the world in the management of technology, strategic management, and the management of ideas and change.

For more about how to liberate your people and transform
your organization through employee ideas,
visit our website at
http://www.ideasarefree.com.

ABOUT BERRETT-KOEHLER PUBLISHERS

Berrett-Koehler is an independent publisher dedicated to an ambitious mission: Creating a World that Works for All.

We believe that to truly create a better world, action is needed at all levels—individual, organizational, and societal. At the individual level, our publications help people align their lives and work with their deepest values. At the organizational level, our publications promote progressive leadership and management practices, socially responsible approaches to business, and humane and effective organizations. At the societal level, our publications advance social and economic justice, shared prosperity, sustainable development, and new solutions to national and global issues.

We publish groundbreaking books focused on each of these levels. To further advance our commitment to positive change at the societal level, we have recently expanded our line of books in this area and are calling this expanded line "BK Currents."

A major theme of our publications is "Opening Up New Space." They challenge conventional thinking, introduce new points of view, and offer new alternatives for change. Their common quest is changing the underlying beliefs, mindsets, institutions, and structures that keep generating the same cycles of problems, no matter who our leaders are or what improvement programs we adopt.

We strive to practice what we preach—to operate our publishing company in line with the ideas in our books. At the core of our approach is stewardship, which we define as a deep sense of responsibility to administer the company for the benefit of all of our "stakeholder" groups: authors, customers, employees, investors, service providers, and the communities and environment around us. We seek to establish a partnering relationship with each stakeholder that is open, equitable, and collaborative.

We are gratified that thousands of readers, authors, and other friends of the company consider themselves to be part of the "BK Community." We hope that you, too, will join our community and connect with us through the ways described on our website at www.bkconnection.com.

BE CONNECTED

Visit Our Website

Go to www.bkconnection.com to read exclusive previews and excerpts of new books, find detailed information on all Berrett-Koehler titles and authors, browse subject-area libraries of books, and get special discounts.

Subscribe to Our Free E-Newsletter

Be the first to hear about new publications, special discount offers, exclusive articles, news about bestsellers, and more! Get on the list for our free e-newsletter by going to www.bkconnection.com.

Participate in the Discussion

To see what others are saying about our books and post your own thoughts, check out our blogs at www.bkblogs.com.

Get Quantity Discounts

Berrett-Koehler books are available at quantity discounts for orders of ten or more copies. Please call us toll-free at (800) 929-2929 or email us at bkp.orders@aidcvt.com.

Host a Reading Group

For tips on how to form and carry on a book reading group in your workplace or community, see our website at www.bkconnection.com.

Join the BK Community

Thousands of readers of our books have become part of the "BK Community" by participating in events featuring our authors, reviewing draft manuscripts of forthcoming books, spreading the word about their favorite books, and supporting our publishing program in other ways. If you would like to join the BK Community, please contact us at bkcommunity@bkpub.com.